LYME PARK

Cheshire

National Trust

Acknowledgements

This guidebook draws on the previous edition, written by Merlin Waterson and revised by Belinda Cousens, and is also heavily indebted to the extensive research among the Legh papers undertaken by Evelyn, Lady Newton at the turn of the 20th century. The writer is also grateful to all those who have given him help in compiling this new edition and, in particular, to Claire Joures for her stoic support throughout. Chattels were accepted in lieu of Inheritance Tax by HM Government and allocated to the National Trust for display at Lyme Park, 2009 and 2010.

James Rothwell

Photographs: B.T. Batsford Ltd p.25; National Trust pp.10, 33, 35, 48, 49 (left), 51, 56; National Trust/Nadia Mackenzie p.23; National Trust Images/Matthew Anthrobus front cover, pp.5, 6, 7, 8; NT Images/Andreas von Einsiedel pp.9, 12, 14, 16, 18, 19, 21, 22, 28, 30, 32, 38; NT Images/John Hammond pp.1, 4, 11, 13, 17, 26, 34, 41, 47, 49 (right), 50, 52, 54, 55, back cover; NT Images/Nick Meers pp.42, 43, 44–5, 45; *Stockport Advertiser* p.29; Robert Thrift p.20.

High-quality prints from the extensive and unique collections of the National Trust Images are available at www.ntprints.com

First published in Great Britain in 1998 by the National Trust

© 1998 The National Trust

Registered charity no. 205846

Reprinted 2003, 2010, 2011; revised 1999, 2000, 2004, 2007, 2008, 2009

ISBN 978-1-84359-114-6

Designed and typeset by James Shurmer (01 11)

Printed by Pureprint Group for National Trust (Enterprises) Ltd, Heelis, Kemble Drive, Swindon, Wilts SN2 2NA on Cocoon Silk made from 100% recycled paper

(*Front cover*) Close view of the south front of Lyme Park showing the massive Ionic portico

(*Title-page*) The Legh augmentation of honour in the plasterwork ceiling of the Library commemorates the rescuing of the Black Prince's standard at the Battle of Crécy in 1346

(*Back cover*) The Legh family coat of arms on the Minton floor tiles in the Orangery

CONTENTS

LYME PARK

Passing under the entrance arch into Lyme's central courtyard, you seem to have stepped into a Renaissance *palazzo* in northern Italy. It looks all of a piece, but in fact hides a great house that has developed gradually since the Middle Ages. The man who commissioned the courtyard in the 1720s was the twelfth of thirteen Peter or Piers Leghs to own Lyme during the family's 550-year tenure. He transformed the exterior of the house, but he left much of the interior as he had found it, because he shared the family's growing reverence for its ancestors and for the ancientness of Lyme.

The intense pride of the Leghs in their past stemmed from the grant of Lyme by Richard II in 1398 to the first Piers Legh and his wife Margaret as a reward for the heroic deeds in battle of her grandfather, Sir Thomas Danyers. The Leghs themselves were present at many of the major battles of the 15th and 16th centuries, and when not campaigning, they hunted the stag. Lyme's indigenous herd of red deer probably encouraged the Leghs to make this their main home from the late 16th century.

Sir Piers VII largely rebuilt Lyme during Elizabeth I's reign: his classical frontispiece survives in the centre of the north range. In the early 17th

century Sir Peter IX completed the work, as well as putting in place the bones of the present garden. The house, garden and park received considerable further attention from Richard Legh in the 1660s and 1670s, and it was for his son, Peter XII, a resolute supporter of the exiled Stuarts, that Giacomo Leoni added the weighty south front with its Ionic portico and so effectively disguised the irregularity of the central courtyard.

Thomas Legh, who inherited Lyme in 1797, was one of the most remarkable members of the family. By the time he came of age in 1814 he had already followed the Nile into parts of Nubia previously unexplored by Europeans, and the following year he was present at the Battle of Waterloo. He also became a well-known Egyptologist and collector of antiquities, modernised the estate farms, exploited the industrial potential of his Lancashire lands and had Lyme itself restored and extensively, but sympathetically, altered by Lewis Wyatt. Thomas Legh's nephew and successor, William John Legh, created the garden much as we see it today and was elevated to the peerage as Lord Newton in 1892 as a reward for a lengthy military and political career.

In the early 20th century, during the tenure of the 2nd Lord Newton, Lyme enjoyed an Indian summer, which is charmingly recorded by his daughter Phyllis in her book *Treasure on Earth*. The burden of upkeep, however, had become so onerous by the end of the Second World War that the 3rd Lord Newton gave Lyme and nearly 1,400 acres of park and moorland to the National Trust in 1946 in order to secure its future. In the absence of an endowment, it was leased to Stockport Corporation (later Metropolitan Borough Council), which maintained it until 1994, undertaking extensive structural repairs. Stockport MBC continues to provide financial support to the National Trust, which now manages Lyme directly.

'Lion', one of the famous Lyme mastiffs (Grand Staircase)

(Right) The Palladian courtyard

TOUR OF THE HOUSE

The Exterior

THE APPROACH AND THE FORECOURT

From the Swineground (car-park) the formal approach to Lyme climbs a steep hill, crossing the site of the old stable block demolished in the 1860s, swings sharply to the right on converging with the north drive and ends up in front of the arched entrance to the forecourt. The somewhat squat gate-piers (which contain sentry boxes and until the late 19th century sported French hunting horns for visitors to announce their arrival) and the massive iron railings are part of Lewis Wyatt's recasting of Lyme after 1813. Until the early 18th century there was a smaller, walled enclosure, the late 17th-century gate-piers of which are now on the A6, at the entrance to the park.

THE NORTH FRONT

The north front clearly illustrates the complex development of Lyme. At its centre is the exuberant Elizabethan frontispiece, which was executed for Sir Piers Legh VII in about 1570 and is one of the earliest instances in England of the classical orders being superimposed on a tower in this way. There are strong similarities in the detail to old Somerset House in London, built twenty years earlier, but the mason was sufficiently provincial to disregard the rules of classical architecture, particularly by placing a column above the middle of the central pediment. The coat of arms within the pediment was added later in the 16th century, and a turret clock had been introduced by the late 17th century.

The lead rainwater heads beneath the heavy parapet are decorated with the arms and monogram

The forecourt and the north front

of Richard and Elizabeth Legh and dated 1676, in which year sash-windows (then very much a novelty) were introduced to the four first-floor windows to the left of the frontispiece. Peter Legh XII extended sashes to the whole façade, added the lead statue of Minerva set in an open pediment over the frontispiece and encased the end bays, accentuating them with giant Corinthian pilasters which rise the height of two floors. The work was undertaken in about 1710, probably by John Platt, a local mason who, with his brothers, was later to execute Giacomo Leoni's designs for Lyme.

THE COURTYARD

In stark contrast to the frontispiece, under which the visitor passes to enter the house, Leoni's Palladian courtyard has all the measured austerity of a north Italian *palazzo*. Heavily rusticated arcades support the *piano nobile*, or principal floor, which is articulated by severe Doric pilasters. To the east, a double flight of steps, with ironwork by the Derbyshire smith John Gardom, leads up to a giant Doric portal which Leoni had intended to be surmounted and flanked by statues. On the north (near) side behind the arcade can be seen the partly blocked doors and mullioned windows of the Elizabethan and Stuart mansion which was being disguised.

Leoni's drawings for the courtyard (two of which survive) were sent in August 1726, and, according to the steward's accounts, work was underway the following year. It was largely complete by 1734, when payments were made for the 'Great Stone Stair Case', although paving was not laid until 1738. The oval basin on the steps, of Hopton stone, was supplied the same year. The only subsequent alterations were the addition of Lewis Wyatt's attic tower above the south (far) side and the Edwardian introduction of pink and white chequered paving, to simulate marble, together with the Italian Renaissance well-head with its finely cut lettering. The mismatched cast-iron urns to either side of the entrance door are mid-19th-century, and the massive fire ladder in the south entrance, which was in use until the 1960s, is late 19th-century.

The east, south and west fronts, described below, can be seen from the garden.

The Elizabethan frontispiece

The south front

THE EAST FRONT

The bay windows, originally Elizabethan, were rebuilt in 1680, that to the right being re-sited from the dais end of the Great Hall to the Drawing Room to allow for the projection of Richard Legh's New Parlour (see p. 17). Lewis Wyatt filled in the bottom terrace and rebuilt the east-front rooms at a higher level between 1814 and 1818. His design reflected the character of the 17th-century work but vastly improved the aspect and lighting of the rooms, which had previously been 'immured by the darksome approximation of garden walls'. The lead statues of Diana and Meleager above the lower parapet were probably supplied by Andries Carpentiere at the same time as two of those on the south front, which came to Lyme from London in 1732.

THE SOUTH FRONT

Leoni's monumental south front, constructed between 1729 and 1732, is more purely Italian than most English Palladian architecture. The giant pilasters that break up the fifteen-bay façade recall Palladio's town houses and the famous west front of another great northern house, Chatsworth. Leoni proposed a cupola to rise behind the massive Ionic portico, but this was rejected by Peter Legh XII, and the pediment remained uncomfortably divorced from the roof behind until Lewis Wyatt added the tower around 1817. The pediment is surmounted by an imposing lead figure of Neptune, flanked by Venus with her magic girdle and Pan with his pipes. One of these must be the large statue 'now sit upon the Great ... pediment', which was mentioned in the steward's accounts in January 1733 and was brought to Lyme by wagon team from Bank Quay, near Warrington, 25 miles away.

THE WEST FRONT

On 19 October 1725 Leoni wrote that he was enclosing 'a rough Draft for ye South Front, which I think will sufficiently shew the nature of ye angle of the West front'. The window architraves, scrolls and cornices are of the same design as those in Leoni's courtyard, and the giant voussoirs of the doorway, similar to his gateways at Stowe, are typical of the Venetian architect at his most austere. The façade, however, has a distinctly provincial air, particularly when compared with the sophistication of the south front and the courtyard, and two letters written in the summer of 1725 make it clear that Leoni's adjustments were to an existing design and were themselves subject to alteration.

The Interior

THE ENTRANCE HALL

This grand classical space is principally the creation of Leoni, between 1732 and 1735. Leoni was largely working within the confines of the Elizabethan Great Hall and disguised the asymmetry of the room – with its entrance and fireplace off-centre – by introducing a monumental screen of columns, designed to be Corinthian, but executed as fluted Ionic. Full-length portraits were set up at both ends of the room of Edward III and the Black Prince, to whom the Leghs ultimately owed Lyme. The 18th-century visitor was thus immediately reminded of the ancientness of the family and their loyalty to the throne, or at least, as Jacobites, to the rightful occupants of the throne.

The portrait of the Black Prince survives and swings out from the wall to reveal the squint from the Elizabethan Great Chamber (now the Drawing Room). This device, which Sir Walter Scott borrowed for his Civil War romance *Woodstock*, is a remarkably imaginative piece of invention by Lewis Wyatt, who remodelled the room in the early 19th century. Wyatt blocked up the access to the 17th-century Stag and New Parlours and centralised the fireplace, providing an exuberantly antiquarian surround with plumed helmets and massive, two-handed swords. This Regency tribute to the Middle Ages was done away with, together with the portrait of Edward III, by the fashionable Edwardian decorators Philippe and Amadée Joubert, who were called in by Lady Newton in 1903. They introduced the present chimneypiece (based on that in the Drawing Room) and installed the three outstanding Mortlake tapestries, which, until the mid-19th century, had hung in the State Bedroom and Dressing Room. A painted sky on the ceiling, which survives under later lining paper, was part of the Joubert scheme.

The room was probably used most extensively in the early 20th century, for the daily reading of prayers, for after-dinner games and conversation, and for the Servants' Ball on New Year's Eve.

The Entrance Hall

According to Phyllis Sandeman, it 'made a perfect ballroom', and the balls were enlightened affairs compared with those of other great houses: the family and their guests always attended, and all the servants were included.

The Jouberts' rich scheme of dark-oak graining, picked out by gilding, was replaced by the present grey-green in 1972, under the guidance of John Fowler. Otherwise, the room is little changed.

PICTURES

CLOCKWISE FROM ENTRANCE DOOR:

ENGLISH, early 18th-century
Peter Legh the Elder (XII) (1669–1744)
Son of Richard Legh and Elizabeth Chicheley; married his cousin Frances Legh in 1687. He was imprisoned in the Tower for his part in the Lancashire Plot of 1694, but was later acquitted. He commissioned Leoni to create this room.

After JAN VAN BELCAMP (d. *c*.1652), early 18th-century
Edward, The Black Prince (1330–76)
The son of Edward III. Because Sir Thomas Danyers had rescued the Black Prince's standard at the siege of Caen and saved his life at the Battle of Crécy, both in 1346, the land on which Lyme was built was granted to his granddaughter,

Margaret, and her husband, Piers Legh I, in 1398. Copied from a portrait now at Windsor for Peter XII.

ENGLISH, early 18th-century
Frances Legh of Bruch (1670–1728)
Wife of Peter XII and daughter and heiress of Piers Legh of Bruch.

OVER CHIMNEYPIECE:

UNKNOWN, *c*.1800
Sir Peter Legh IX (1563–1636)
Inherited Lyme in 1589 and continued the rebuilding started by his grandfather. He was knighted in 1598 on his return from fighting with the Earl of Leicester in the Netherlands. This is a late copy of a portrait painted *c*.1591.

TAPESTRIES
From *Hero and Leander* series
Mortlake, 1625–36
Although an incomplete set, these are widely held to be among the most important English tapestries in the country. They were designed by Francis Cleyn, who was appointed designer to the Mortlake factory in 1625, and bear the marks of Philip de Maecht, the master weaver, and Sir Francis Crane, first director of the factory, who died in 1636.

The Entrance Hall in 1900, when it still contained Wyatt's chimneypiece topped with plumed helmets

'Haste to the Wedding'
painted by Phyllis
Sandeman, c.1908,
in the Entrance Hall

The tragic story of *Hero and Leander* concerns two lovers separated by the waters of the Helle-spont (the straits between the Aegean and the Black Sea). Hero, priestess of Aphrodite at Sestos, inspired the love of Leander, who swam out to her from Abydos, a town on the opposite, Asian shore. On a tempestuous night Leander was drowned and Hero threw herself into the sea in despair. The scenes illustrated here are, from the left of the fireplace: *Leander Swimming from Abydos, The Arrival of Leander at Hero's Tower* and *The Meeting of Hero and Leander.* The fourth in the set (now at the V&A) depicts *Hero Mourning the Loss of Leander.*

FURNITURE

The fine seat furniture is all English and mainly mid-18th-century. The smaller of the two sofas, upholstered in yellow silk damask and on elegant cabriole legs, is slightly later in date and is part of a set which includes five armchairs, one of which is alongside, upholstered in maroon velvet. The grained and parcel-gilt hall-chair of *c.*1700, to the left of the fireplace, must have been part of a set. Flanking the portrait of the Black Prince

are two chairs incorporating the arms of Peter Legh XIII and his wife, Martha Benet. They are mid-18th-century in style but were probably made in the 1820s.

The Louis XIV-style giltwood side-tables and three-branch giltwood girandoles, both sporting the ram's head crest of the Leghs, are Edwardian and were introduced in 1903 as part of the Joubert remodel-ling. The yew chest-on-stand is late 17th-century.

Grand piano by Erard, London, 1870, veneered in burr-walnut.

METALWORK

*Two-tier ormolu chandelier, c.*1825, introduced by Thomas Legh and shown in an 1840 lithograph of the room.

Pair of pierced brass andirons decorated with stylised flower heads, *c.*1670. These are probably the 'andirons of brasse' recorded as being in the 'Greate Dining Room' in 1687.

CARPET

Large Axminster carpet, the design attributed to A.W.N. Pugin, which was woven for the drawing-room of Abney Hall, Cheadle, *c.*1852, as part of the lavish J.G. Crace scheme.

CLOCKS

ON MANTELSHELF:

Eight-day English striking spring clock in mahogany case by Moses Nicholason, London, *c.*1780.

BENEATH PORTRAIT OF BLACK PRINCE:

Eight-day English musical table clock in japanned and silver-mounted case, by John Berry, London, *c.*1735. Six tunes are played on twelve bells.

Leave by the double doors at the right-hand end of the window wall and ascend a short flight of stairs to the Drawing Room.

THE DRAWING ROOM

The rich ornament of this essentially Elizabethan and Jacobean room is in stark contrast to the Entrance Hall, and reveals the hidden antiquity of the house as well as its piecemeal internal development. The room would have served originally as a great chamber where the family could eat away from the bustle of the Great Hall. Although still described as 'the Greate Dining Room' in the 1687 inventory, by then it had already been partly superseded by Richard Legh's New Parlour and its use must have been limited still further by the creation of the Saloon in the early 18th century. In the mid-18th century the room was painted 'dead white'. Access was made considerably easier by Lewis Wyatt in the early 19th century, when the room

The Drawing Room

*(Above) A romanticised view of the Drawing Room
in Tudor times; coloured lithograph from Joseph Nash's*
Mansions of England in the Olden Time *(1849)*

came into its own again as a drawing-room,
boosted in importance by the family's increased
interest in the Elizabethan elements of the house.
Wyatt probably designed the hinged panels, which
open to reveal the view down into the Entrance
Hall, and his decoration survives largely intact.
Wyatt's squint took the place of a buffet niche,
possibly that now in the Stone Parlour (ticket
office). The sombre and archaic character of the
room is further enhanced by the dim light cast
through the fine, partly medieval stained glass,
which was gathered here at the same time.

FIREPLACE

The plaster overmantel bears the arms of Elizabeth
I flanked by atlantes and caryatids, whose full bellies
represent plenty. Its awkwardness in relation to the

plaster frieze and ceiling suggests it was moved here
from elsewhere in the house, probably in the late
17th century, when the chimneypiece beneath is
likely to have been made. The two parts of the fireplace were perhaps brought together here for the
Duke of York's visit in 1676.

The fine pierced steel basket-grate, matching
fender and fire-irons were made c.1785.

PLASTERWORK

The plasterwork is probably early 17th-century
and may well have been undertaken by the same
team which worked on the Great Chamber at
Dorfold Hall, near Nantwich, c.1616. The intricate
strapwork pattern of the ceiling is unusual in having
a distinct central feature, from which the chandelier
now hangs. Each of the grotesque masks in the
frieze is different except for four repeats, which
were added to fill gaps left by the construction of
the bay in 1680 and the sashes c.1710.

PANELLING

The arcaded oak wainscotting is early 17th-century and is inlaid with holly and bog oak. It may have been made for another of the Leghs' houses, Bradley in Lancashire. In 1748 Peter XIII refers to 'the Bradley Wainscot' and mentions both the 'Eating Parlour and the Drawing Room' as potential recipients. (Either name could have been used for the Drawing Room in the mid-18th century.) Wyatt inserted the door to the Stag Parlour and the pilasters either side of the bay, and probably also applied the dark varnish to the panelling.

The ebony cabinet and Chinoiserie wall-light, c.1760, are flanked by mid-18th-century chairs, which retain their original upholstery, and stand against the early 17th-century panelling

STAINED GLASS

The stained glass almost certainly includes elements of the 'three large windows glaz'd with old armorial bearings' recorded in Disley church by Lord Torrington in 1790 and removed to Lyme in the early 19th century. There are medieval fragments, undoubtedly of ecclesiastical origin, 16th- and 17th-century armorials relating to the Leghs and, in the bay, a fine collection of late 16th-century panels depicting the arms of the Garter Knights during the reign of Elizabeth I. Alongside these are more domestic subjects, including portraits of Sir Peter IX and an exceptionally fine late 17th-century series of the Twelve Sibyls and the labours of the months. The last series was produced by Flemish glaziers.

PICTURES

IN BAY:

The set of six early 18th-century small oval portraits represents the Stuart monarchs, including Mary, Queen of Scots and Queen Anne, but not the 'usurping' William and Mary, as might be expected of a Jacobite house.

OPPOSITE FIREPLACE AND WINDOWS:

The 17th-century portraits of Stuart courtiers in gilt and silvered frames are on loan from the National Portrait Gallery and compare to those which were hanging in the room from the early 19th century to 1946. That to the right of the entrance door is by Cornelius Johnson of *Sir Robert Cotton, 1st Bt*, whilst those to the left, by an unknown artist, are of *Anthony Hamilton*, a prominent Jacobite, and his brother, *Sir George Hamilton*. On the wall opposite the windows are (from left to right) three portraits by Sir Peter Lely of *Henry Howard, 6th Duke of Norfolk, Anne Hyde, Duchess of York* and *Anna Maria Brudenell, Countess of Shrewsbury* and one by Sir Godfrey Kneller, purportedly of *Henry Sidney, Earl of Romney*.

FURNITURE

In 1687 the 'Great Dining Room' was predominantly furnished with chairs. It still is, but they are now mostly mid-18th-century, like much of the other furniture. The three carved giltwood girandoles of *c.*1760, with their delicate Chinoiserie design including ho-ho bird finials, were converted to electricity in 1903, when the mother-of-pearl shades were introduced. The carved giltwood chandelier of *c.*1750 is one of a suite of three in the house. Between the windows hangs a pair of carved and gilt pier-glasses, *c.*1730, above slightly earlier tables with Chinese lacquer tops. The rosewood sofa-table is of *c.*1800 and the possibly Indian, rosewood tripod-table of *c.*1830.

CERAMICS

BETWEEN THE WINDOWS:

Pair of Meissen candelabra, late 19th-century.

AGAINST THE WEST WALL:

Chinese blue-and-white beaker vase, and slender baluster vase and cover, both Kangxi, *c.*1700.

CARPETS

Kouba floral carpet, 17th-century.

Large Heriz carpet with the usual angular medallion and spandrels, late 19th-century.

CLOCK

Eight-day English musical striking spring clock in tortoiseshell veneered case, by Nathaniel Barnes, London, *c.*1760.

THE STAG PARLOUR

It was in this room that the Jacobite 'Cheshire Gentlemen' met to plot the return of the exiled Stuarts in the 1690s and it was here in 1745 that the club was finally disbanded after Peter XIII had reputedly persuaded his co-conspirators not to risk supporting the Young Pretender's ill-fated rising. Perhaps because of this tradition of dangerous intrigue, gentlemen diners traditionally retired to the Stag Parlour for port rather than remaining in the more public Dining Room.

The Stag Parlour, as it is seen today, is almost entirely early 19th-century. Sir Peter IX's early 17th-century 'Little Parlour' was reconstructed by Wyatt to bring it up to the level of the Drawing Room and his new Dining Room and Library. Wyatt incorporated elements of the original overmantel, including the oak lower section with its gallery of thin Ionic columns, and he probably based the plasterwork on what had existed. The overmantel contains a highly conjectural representation of the house prior to the Elizabethan rebuilding, and the frieze, from which the room takes its name, depicts the life of a stag. Most of Wyatt's detail was at least vaguely Jacobean, apart from his fire surround, which was replaced with the present, more convincing stone pastiche by the Jouberts, *c.*1904. The wall-hangings and curtains have recently been renewed, replicating the early 19th-century scheme.

PICTURES

To the right of the fireplace are portraits of *Charles II* in the manner of Sir Peter Lely, and *Prince James Edward*, the Old Pretender, from the studio of Alexis Simon Belle. Above the entrance door is *James Stuart, 1st Duke of Richmond and 4th Duke of Lennox*, attributed to Theodore Russel, and above the Dining Room door, *Charles I*, after Van Dyck.

TAPESTRIES

The Building of Thebes and *Cadmus sent in search of Europa* from the *Cadmus* series. Antwerp, Michael Wauters in the style of Daniel Janssens, 1670s. The three tapestries from the Cadmus series at Lyme (see also Ante-Room) are a rare survival in England of a set once common in country houses here. Cadmus was the legendary founder of the ancient Greek city of Thebes.

FURNITURE

*Four from a set of six mahogany open armchairs, c.*1820, the intricately pierced splats incorporating the monogram of Charles I and the seats upholstered in 17th-century embroidered silk, reputed to have been part of the cloak worn by the King on the scaffold. The Leghs displayed here all their Royalist relics, which in 1879 also included a silver-mounted dagger and a pair of gloves, said to have belonged to King Charles I, and a 'Bas relief ... of "the Salutation" in ancient needlework frame' – presumably that ascribed elsewhere to Mary, Queen of Scots.

An oak and fruitwood court cupboard, early 17th-century, and *a Flemish oak draw-leaf table*, early 17th-century.

(Overleaf) The Stag Parlour

The Stag Parlour

THE DINING ROOM

In 1680 John Platt entered into a contract with Richard Legh 'to do all ye masons worke of a new parler' and it was for this New or Great Parlour that Grinling Gibbons supplied carvings. It served as the principal dining-room, but by the early 19th century was too small to cope with the burgeoning scale of entertainment of the period, and in 1814 the whole projecting block was rebuilt for Thomas Legh, to designs by Lewis Wyatt. As with the Stag Parlour, Wyatt raised the floor level. He also enlarged the room by adding the deep bay window and incorporating a wide corridor adjoining the Stag Parlour.

Although Wyatt drastically replanned the room, he showed great sensitivity to its earlier decoration, adopting the rich motifs of the late 17th century for the exuberant plasterwork of the walls and ceiling. The heavy swags, festoons and elaborate frieze were oak-grained to appear as if carved, and an actual 17th-century piece of carving – probably by Gibbons and similar to his famous Kirtlington panel – was incorporated over the fireplace. The Jouberts redecorated the room c.1905 using pale greens, buffs and pinks à la Robert Adam, but in 1979 it was regrained, with the ceiling a flat white, as intended by Wyatt. The crimson and silk damask curtains were rewoven in 2004, following a pattern used at Lyme in the mid-19th century.

The table is set for dinner, c.1905 – to be served à la Française with some elements of the more modish à la Russe for convenience. The setting is deliberately old-fashioned, in keeping with the antiquarian attitudes of the 2nd Lord Newton and his wife. The host and hostess, sitting at either end of the table, would serve the soup and the fish respectively, the plates being handed round by liveried footmen under the eye of the butler. Silver tureens are already on the table for the second and remove courses (usually roast meats), and the console table at the far end is set up for the beginning of the meal. There are extra glasses, condiments and cutlery, together with wine decanters, silver-gilt cutlery for the dessert course and a large silver cup-and-cover for display.

PICTURES

The historic hang, introduced by Wyatt and consisting of three-quarter-length portraits of Stuart courtiers and 17th- and 18th-century members of

The decorative radiator covers in the Dining Room were introduced by the Jouberts in 1908

the family, has recently been recreated with the help of loans from the National Portrait Gallery.

FLANKING STAG PARLOUR DOOR:

JAMES FELLOWS (active 1711–51)
Martha Benet, Mrs Legh (d.1787)
Painted three years before her marriage to Peter XIII in 1737.

Sir PETER LELY (1618–80)
Sir Edward Nicholas (d.1669)

FIREPLACE WALL, FROM RIGHT:

? Sir PETER LELY (1618–80)
Richard Legh (1634–87), 1667
He inherited Lyme in 1643 and undertook extensive improvements to the house after the Restoration.

Sir PETER LELY (1618–80) and studio
? Elizabeth Chicheley, Mrs Legh (d.1728)
She married Richard Legh in 1661, bore him thirteen children and outlived him by over 40 years.

(Above) The Dining Room

School of Sir PETER LELY (1618–80)
Anne Coventry, Lady Savile (d. 1667)
The step-mother of Elizabeth Chicheley, she was renowned for having held out against the Parliamentarians at the siege of Sheffield Castle in 1644, while heavily pregnant.

? EDWARD GOUDGE (active 1690–1735)
Sir John Stonhouse, 3rd Bt (1673–1733)
He holds his white wand of office as Comptroller of the Household to Queen Anne.

FLANKING ANTE-ROOM DOOR:

Studio of Sir PETER LELY (1618–80)
Gilbert Sheldon, Bishop of Oxford (1598–1677)

Studio of Sir PETER LELY (1618–80)
Nell Gwyn (1650–87)
Mistress of Charles II.

WINDOW WALL AND BAY, FROM RIGHT:

ENGLISH, early 18th-century
Sir Streynsham Master (1682–1724)
A distinguished naval officer, he married Richard Legh's second daughter Elizabeth.

WEESOP (active 1641–9)
Sir Henry Gage (d. 1644)

Studio of Sir ANTHONY VAN DYCK (1599–1641)
Thomas Wentworth, 1st Earl of Strafford (1593–1641)

After Sir PETER LELY (1618–80)
Formerly known as *James Scott, Duke of Monmouth* (1649–85)

FURNITURE

The Edwardian Chippendale-style chairs were introduced by the Jouberts to replace a set of sabre-leg, or 'Waterloo', chairs supplied for the newly completed room in the early 19th century. Two of the superb Rococo console tables (flanking the Ante-Room door) are mid-18th-century; the other two are thought to be highly convincing early 19th-century copies, produced as part of Wyatt's scheme.

CERAMICS

The table is laid with a tortoiseshell-ground Sèvres dinner service, presented by the French government to the Foreign Secretary, Lord Liverpool, in 1802 to mark the Peace of Amiens. Always known by his family as the 'Napoleon China', it was ordered from the Sèvres factory by France's foreign minister, Talleyrand, and, with the collection of silver, is on loan from Lord Liverpool's descendants.

METALWORK

The silver on the table and sideboard was accumulated between c.1700 and 1850. Of particular note are the two large tureens with handles in the form

The Sèvres dinner service was presented by the French government to the Foreign Secretary, Lord Liverpool, to mark the Peace of Amiens in 1802, and has been loaned to Lyme by his descendants

of eagles, made by Frederick Kandler in 1756, and the Rococo epergne at the centre of the table, made by Emick Romer in 1760. The salts in the form of baskets are by William Brind, 1764, and the Neo-classical cup and cover at the back of the side-table by Thomas Heming, 1769. Although the collection is not from Lyme, it is very similar in style and composition to the silver recorded here in 1879.

CLOCK

Eight-day English striking bracket clock in mahogany case with automated scene in arch depicting two woodmen at work and a man shooting a pheasant, by Stedman of Godalming, c.1785.

THE ANTE-ROOM

Once family and guests had processed through from the Library to the Dining Room, this room would be used as a servery, linked by a staircase behind the south wall to the Kitchen below (not open to visitors). A square of cut boards against the Dining Room wall is the only evidence of a cleverly concealed hoist, installed in the early 19th century to bring up heavier items. Wyatt reused an early 18th-century polished Hopton-stone chimney-piece for the false fireplace in the north-west corner.

PICTURES

Over the doors are portraits of *Major John Hanbury (1664–1734)* and *Margaret Chambre, Mrs George Hanbury-Williams* (m.1768), both by unknown English artists. These pictures, with others in the house, are on loan from the Hanbury-Williams family.

TAPESTRIES

SOUTH WALL:

The Rape of Europa from the *Cadmus* series
Antwerp, 1670s (see p.15 for further details)
Two pieces of carpet have been attached to make the tapestry fit the space, the lower one being a rare survival of cheap, mass-produced Scotch or Kidderminster carpet, which was flat-woven in wool.

DINING-ROOM WALL:

Flora and Eurydice
Brussels, *c.*1700
To the right is Eurydice being bitten by a snake and to the left Flora, the Roman goddess of flowers, sitting in her garden, which was filled with blossom by her husband, Zephyr. The magnificent side borders, showing men in eastern dress, are from one of the *Cadmus* tapestries.

CLOCK

Eight-day English musical clock in a japanned case with a repertoire of seven Jacobite airs, by Claude Viet, London, *c.*1715. Probably acquired by Peter Legh XII who was known for his Jacobite sympathies. The only 18th-century clock at Lyme, apart from the wall clock in the Servants' Hall, that is from the original collection.

THE LIBRARY

Wyatt created the Library in the early 19th century by throwing together the apartments occupied in the late 17th century by Richard Legh. Before then, there had been no room set aside specifically for the family's books. The Leghs had, however, long been collecting them and the Lyme Library contains a number of mediaeval manuscripts as well as an exceptionally interesting group of 15th–17th-century books, many of which can be proved to have been at Lyme since the time that they were published. They are able to tell us much about the earliest period of the house's history and include a 15th-century Missal or prayer book, a Shakespeare Second Folio and a first edition of Sir Walter Raleigh's *Historie of the World*, which was sent to Francis Legh by his old tutor, Ralph Richardson, in 1636. The family's books can be identified by the ram's-head crest stamped on their spines.

DECORATION

Wyatt's 'Jacobethan' ceiling, the massive fireplace and the oak bookcases combine elements of 16th- and 17th-century design but the room is still distinctly 19th century in character and is in the process of being restored to its appearance during the ownership of Thomas Legh, for whom it was created. A rich crimson and gold flock wallpaper will be reprinted for the walls, crimson mohair velvet will be gofraged (stamped) in replication of surviving fragments for the curtains and seat furniture and the ceiling will be returned to its original oak graining, painted out by the Jouberts, *c.*1904. The four elaborate cartouches around the acanthus-leaf centrepiece depict the Leghs' augmentation of honour – the most prized of heraldic distinctions. It was granted to Sir Piers VII by Elizabeth I in 1575 in recognition of the saving of the Black Prince's standard at Crécy and comprises a mailed arm holding a banner against a background of silver stars.

THE CAXTON MISSAL

The jewel of the Library, and of printed books throughout the National Trust's rich collections, is the sole survivor of the earliest known edition of the Sarum Missal (the prayer book for the most

The Library bay in 1889 *by Evelyn, Lady Newton*

significant version of the pre-Reformation English Mass), printed in more than one colour, contains prints from the first woodblocks used in French printing and is the first book in which Caxton used his iconic personal device. The book can be proved to have been owned by the Leghs of Lyme from at least 1508 and it was probably acquired soon after publication by Sir Piers V, who was both a knight and, following his wife's death, also a priest. It may have been intended for the chantry chapel Legh founded at Disley to pray for the souls of family members and its numerous annotations, excisions and deletions are richly evocative of late mediaeval life and of the turbulent times of the English Reformation.

The future of the Caxton Missal at Lyme was secured by its acquisition in March 2008 and, following detailed analysis and the preparation of a suitable display case, it will be on display in the Library from the middle of 2009. This project has been supported by grants from the HLF, the Art Fund, the Pilgrim Trust, the Foyle Foundation, Royal Oak, Friends of the National Libraries, National Trust centres and associations including the Peak District and a number of other organisations and individuals.

PICTURES

Attributed to TILLY KETTLE (1735–86)
Henry Vansittart of Foxley, Berkshire (1732–69)
Third son of Arthur Vansittart of Shottesbrooke; Governor of Bengal 1760–4.

LAURA HOPE (1858–1929), 1906
Richard William Davenport Legh, 3rd Lord Newton (1888–1960)
Owner of Lyme from 1920, he succeeded as 3rd Baron in 1940 and gave Lyme to the National Trust in 1946. He married, in 1914, the Hon. Helen Meysey-Thompson, daughter of the 1st Lord Knaresborough. Laura Hope (née Troubridge) was Lord Newton's cousin and friend and also painted his brother, Piers.

'SPY' (Sir Leslie Ward)
An Imperialist without guile, c.1908
This cartoon of the 2nd Lord Newton, c.1908, is the watercolour original for one of the famous series by 'Spy' which appeared in the magazine *Vanity Fair*.

In the display case on the corner table is a miniature of *Thomas Legh* (1792–1857) by Sir WILLIAM

A fragment of a Classical Greek tombstone. The masks suggest that it commemorates an actor or playwright

CHARLES ROSS (1794–1860), and two early 19th-century micro-mosaic pictures of Lyme, from the north and the south. The watercolour views of Lyme in the 1890s were painted by DULCIBELLA LEGH, known as Sybil (1859–1960), the eldest daughter of the 1st Lord Newton.

SCULPTURE

Thomas Legh's most important discovery whilst in Athens in 1812, a stele (tombstone) of *c.*350 BC depicting an aristocratic Athenian couple, Melisto and Epigenes, is displayed above the chimneypiece. Two other stelae face each other in the window bay; that on the right includes theatrical masks, so probably commemorates a playwright or actor, and that on the left shows Arkesis, a young mother who presumably died in childbirth and holds out her closely swaddled baby before her. The latter is particularly poignant given the death in childbirth in 1831 of Thomas Legh's first wife, Ellen, aged just 21.

FURNITURE

The bookcases were designed by Wyatt, who probably also introduced the giltwood chandelier of *c*.1750. It is *en suite* with those in the Drawing Room and Saloon and may have hung in the New Parlour before that room was dismantled. The octagonal oak library table in the centre of the room and the rectangular oak extending table between the windows were made *c*.1852, possibly to designs by A.W.N. Pugin, as part of the J.G. Crace scheme for Abney Hall. The two chairs upholstered in a linen floral print are English, *c*.1770, and form part of the same set as one of the sofas in the Entrance Hall. The mahogany architect's table, with a pull-out front, rising top and candle-slides, is of *c*.1790. The terrestrial and celestial globes on ebonised frames are dated 1851 and 1853 respectively.

CARPET

Large mid-19th-century Persian carpet with the small-scale 'Herati' design field and multiple borders typical of the 'Khorassan' pattern. The carpet was for many years in Beckford's Library in Bath and was presented to the National Trust in 1997 by James Lees-Milne.

CLOCK

Eight-day quarter-striking bracket clock in a boullework case, signed 'Moisy a Paris', *c*.1750, with matching bracket.

Before viewing the Grand Staircase, the visitor should cross to the Saloon.

THE SALOON

The Saloon was intended as the principal receiving room and so is richly finished as well as being placed centrally, behind the giant columns of the south-front portico. Leoni described his initial scheme in a letter of September 1725: 'ye Sallon is intended to go up two clear storys, and to be finished with a Cupolo, a Portico in ye front ...'. Mrs Legh, however, 'did not approve of it [the cupola] and desired the Front to be built without'. A revised

cross-section, in which the additional storey was also omitted, was enclosed with a letter written the following August, but as there are no references in the accounts to the finishing of the room, it is likely that it was incomplete at Peter XII's death in 1744.

The oak panelling and the composite pilasters are probably of the 1730s, their finely carved detail being comparable to work elsewhere by John Moore of Macclesfield, but much of the rest of the fitting-out was done by Wyatt in the early 19th century. Wyatt almost certainly introduced the Gibbons carvings and at least embellished the Rococo ceiling, which incorporates the mailed arm of the Leghs. He also replaced the original entrance from the Bright Gallery with a fireplace and installed a door into the Grand Staircase with a large plate-glass mirror opposite to create the impression of a continuing *enfilade*, when seen from his new Library. Wyatt's central fireplace was

The limewood carvings in the Saloon are traditionally attributed to the greatest master of the art, Grinling Gibbons

The Saloon

subsequently replaced by the Jouberts, who also reduced the size of the mirror above.

CARVINGS

By long family tradition, the limewood carvings in four festoons (representing the Seasons, Music, the Arts and Science) are by Grinling Gibbons, the greatest master of his art. In November 1684 Sir John Chicheley's visit to 'Mr Gibbons concerned a peece of Carved worke' on behalf of his brother-in-law, Richard Legh. The carvings, which are comparable in quality with Gibbons's undisputed work at Petworth, were probably intended for his New Parlour. When that room was rebuilt as the present Dining Room, Wyatt moved the carvings here, hanging them centrally as trophies rather than surrounding the panels, as would originally have been intended. The carving around the chimney-glass is contemporary but by an inferior hand and was introduced in 1904.

The panelling was restored in 2000 to the colour

intended by Wyatt with the help of funding from the Kensington and Chelsea Association of the National Trust.

FURNITURE

The set of George I walnut chairs and a settee were sold to Peter XII by his niece, Lady Coventry, in 1720. Her husband, the 4th Earl of Coventry, had died the previous year without adequately providing for her, and when the chairs were despatched, she wrote: 'I am ashamed to say there is a price to them (25 guineas) … but as the Lord of Lyme is so farr a richer and potent person than me, poor Widow I am forced to name the sum, but you are as free to send them back and no harm done.'

The giltwood chandelier of *c.*1750 is the last of the suite of three at Lyme. The mirrors and scagliola-topped pier-tables between the windows are early 19th-century but convincingly mid-18th-century in style. They were probably introduced by Wyatt, together with the giltwood window pelmets.

MUSICAL INSTRUMENT

Walnut harpsichord, signed by John Hitchcock of London, mid-1760s. This is one of his earliest known instruments.

CLOCK

Eight-day English musical clock with automated scene depicting two musicians playing and a man dancing a jig, by Eardley Norton, London, *c.*1780.

THE GRAND STAIRCASE

The Grand Staircase was formed at least partly out of the space occupied by its 17th-century predecessor, up which fourteen Dutch troopers ascended in July 1694 to arrest Peter XII on suspicion of complicity in the Jacobite 'Lancashire Plot'. Payments for work on the new staircase were made between 1734 and 1736, the joinery almost certainly being designed and produced by John Moore. The heavily sculpted ceiling was executed by two otherwise little-known plasterers, Francis Conseiglio and Joseph Palfreman. The landing leading to the Long Gallery is supported on square Corinthian pillars with finely carved limewood capitals.

DECORATION

In 1998 the Grand Staircase was redecorated to return it to the bright red with rich, dark joinery which had existed from the late 19th century until 1946, when the house was given to the National Trust. The Grand Staircase and Bright Gallery are treated as one, as they always were. In the early 19th century the walls of both were ointment pink, and prior to that they had been light blue, deep blue-green and – in the early 18th century – donkey grey.

PICTURES

The present hang is based on that recorded in 19th- and early 20th-century illustrations and contains the few subject pictures in a collection predominantly made up of portraits. Also gathered together here is an important group of paintings by a mysterious portraitist known only by his monogram 'J.H.'. He practised in the north-west in the mid-17th century, primarily amongst Catholic and Jacobite families; there are other examples of his work at Sizergh Castle in Cumbria and Stoneyhurst in Lancashire.

BEHIND THE SCREEN OF PILLARS, FROM THE LEFT:

? JAMES WILLIAM COLE (active 1849–82)
Thomas, 2nd Lord Newton (1857–1942) as a boy with his favourite mastiff, 'Lady'
The 2nd Lord Newton worked in the diplomatic service before entering Parliament as MP for Newton in 1886. He succeeded his father in 1898 and was Paymaster-General in 1915–16. He married Evelyn Bromley Davenport, the author of *House of Lyme*, in 1880. In 1920 he handed Lyme over to his elder son, the future 3rd Lord Newton.

JOHN TRIVETT NETTLESHIP (1841–1902)
'Lion' in the Drawing Room at Lyme
One of the last of the Lyme mastiffs.

ATTILIO BACCANI (exh. 1859–92)
Emily Wodehouse, Lady Newton (d. 1901), 1867
Daughter of the Ven. Charles Wodehouse and wife of the 1st Lord Newton, whom she married in 1856.

GEORGE RICHMOND, RA (1809–96)
William, 1st Lord Newton (1828–98)
MP for Lancashire and later for East Cheshire; created Baron Newton of Newton-in-Makerfield, 1892. This portrait was presented to the 2nd Lord Newton by the estate tenants on his coming-of-age in 1878. He is said to have refused any other gift.

UNDERNEATH STAIRS, FROM LEFT:

ENGLISH, 1795
Thomas Legh (1792–1857) as a child with a Lyme Mastiff
The future owner of Lyme wears a blue sash which is probably taken from the uniform of his father, Thomas Peter Legh, as colonel of the 3rd Lancashire Light Dragoons. On loan from the Hon. Mrs Simon Weinstock, granddaughter of the 3rd Lord Newton.

? After ABRAHAM STORCK (*c.*1635–after 1704)
Shipping off the Coast
Possibly a representation of Charles II's return to England in 1660.

IN ADJOINING GALLERY:

A fine series of early 18th-century full-length portraits, the two nearest the Entrance Hall being of *Anne Master, Countess of Coventry* (1691–1788,

The Grand Staircase
around 1904

the niece of Peter Legh XII – see Saloon), in the manner of Hans Hysing, and *Sir Robert Walpole, 1st Earl of Orford*, Britain's first Prime Minister, from the studio of J.B. van Loo. Those beyond the doorway to the Grand Staircase are of *Robert Vansittart* by Edward Goudge, his brother *Arthur Vansittart* by Michael Dahl and Arthur's wife, *Martha Stonhouse*, by Jonathan Richardson the Elder.

ON STAIRS, IN ASCENDING ORDER:

ENGLISH, mid-17th-century
Keeper Bullock gralloching a Buck
A keeper Bullock (perhaps a descendant) worked at Lyme in the late 18th century.

WILLIAM BRADLEY (1801–57)
Thomas Legh (1792–1857)
An intrepid traveller who twice visited the Near East and was among the first Englishmen to penetrate as far as Nubia. Despite being illegitimate, he inherited Lyme on his father's death in 1797 and employed Wyatt in 1813 to remodel the house. He is shown in eastern dress, which he wore in 1818 in order to investigate sites around the Dead Sea in safety. He and his companions, who included William Bankes of Kingston Lacy, assumed eastern names, Legh's being 'Osman'. His Nubian servant is shown on the right.

ENGLISH, *c.*1724. Signed *Benedictus*
Francis Legh (1685/6–1737)
The 6th son of Richard Legh, he fought in the War of the Spanish Succession but was not, in spite of the naval references in this painting and family tradition, an admiral. The map is of Margate Sands.

MASTER J.H. (active 1647–66)
A Grey Stallion and Attendant
In the 1879 inventory recorded as 'Richard Legh (with white horse as page to Charles II)'. Given that the picture is dated 1666, this is unlikely. A representation of the park building known as the Cage before it was rebuilt by Leoni is included in the top-left corner.

After Sir PETER PAUL RUBENS (1577–1640)
Salome with the Head of John the Baptist

MASTER J.H. (active 1647–66)
Bacchic Procession of Putti, 1660

MASTER J.H. (active 1647–66)
Piers Legh of Bruch (1637–71)
Grandson of Sir Peter IX and father of Frances, wife of Peter XII. He was involved in the Royalist rising under Sir George Booth, put down at Winnington Bridge in 1659.

MASTER J.H. (active 1647–66)
Richard Legh (1634–87)
Inherited Lyme in 1643. Under the Commonwealth he was MP for Cheshire and after the Restoration was Lord Lieutenant of Cheshire and Deputy Lieutenant of Lancashire. He created a

suite of new rooms in the north range and commissioned the Gibbons carvings.

? ITALIAN, 18th-century
The Bay of Naples

MASTER J.H. (active 1647–66)
Thomas Legh (1636–97)
Brother of Richard Legh and the second surviving son of Dr Thomas Legh. Signed and dated 1662.

MASTER J.H. (active 1647–66)
Elizabeth Chicheley, Mrs Legh (d. 1728)
Daughter of Sir Thomas Chicheley of Wimpole and wife of Richard Legh.

JOHN SLACK, mid-18th-century
Joseph Watson (1648–1753), 1750
He was keeper at Lyme from 1674 and was reputedly still hunting the stag at the age of 102, when this portrait was painted.

R. MILLAN after DIEGO VELÁZQUEZ (1599–1660)
Las Meninas
The mastiff shown in Velázquez's famous self-portrait with the Spanish royal family and their attendants is reputedly one of the Lyme breed. A pair was presented to Philip III of Spain by James I in 1604. The Lyme mastiffs were renowned for

their size, and tradition relates that one accompanied Sir Peter II into battle at Agincourt in 1415. They became extinct shortly after the First World War.

ON LANDING:

ENGLISH, 17th-century
Bird's-eye View of Lyme, c.1690
The house is seen as embellished by Richard Legh and before Leoni's early 18th-century remodelling. This is a fragment of a picture recorded in Neale's *Views of Seats* (1824) as 'A White Horse, very large, with a View of Lyme Hall in its ancient state …'.

ENGLISH, 18th-century, manner of JAN WYCK (1645–1700)
A Staghunt
Appears to show the curious Lyme custom whereby stags were driven through the Stag Pond (no longer existing) at mid-summer. The Leghs' passion for hunting red deer is described in Walter Scott's *Peveril of the Peak*.

MASTER J.H. (active 1647–66)
Anne Venables, Mrs Leveson
The daughter of Peter Venables of Kinderton and the second cousin of Francis Legh of Lyme. She married Francis Fowler who subsequently took the name of Leveson.

FURNITURE

A carved and grained Rococo console table with white marble top, *c.*1745, originally painted a stone colour.

Two from a set of six mahogany side-chairs upholstered in pink floral damask on acanthus-carved cabriole legs, *c.*1750.

ON LANDING:

A black and gilt lacquer cushion-framed and crested mirror with Chinoiserie decoration, *c.*1690.

METALWORK

A bronze hexagonal lantern with etched glass sides and smoke hood, *c.*1820.

(Left) A Grey Stallion and Attendant; by a mid-17th-century artist known only by his initials 'J.H.'. Several of his paintings hang on the Grand Staircase

CLOCKS

Eight-day English musical clock in mahogany case with brass mounts, automated scene of troops going into battle and four tunes, by Wagstaffe, London, *c.*1780.

Eight-day English longcase clock in walnut case by Edward Avenell, London, *c.*1720.

TROPHIES

A moose's head, probably shot by 1st Lord Newton, and *the head of one of the last of Lyme's wild white cattle*, which became extinct in the 1880s.

THE LONG GALLERY

The Long Gallery was used in the traditional way for gentle exercise in bad weather and to display family portraits, but it has also been the setting for the family's theatricals. Evelyn, Lady Newton came from a long line of enthusiastic amateur actors, and each Christmas, from the late 19th century until the First World War, a play would be put on involving all the family with the exception of Lord Newton, who, according to his daughter Phyllis, 'could be counted on to throw plenty of cold water'. The actors would be rehearsed by Lady Newton's brother, William Bromley Davenport, who had his own private theatre at Capesthorne, near Congleton. Also at Christmas, Lady Newton would dispense presents to the children of the estate here, in strict order of age, from the youngest upwards. Two hundred years earlier, Sir Peter IX had sat in the 'compas window of his gallerie' to hear the claims and complaints of his tenants.

With its fine early 17th-century oak panelling, which is similar to that in the Drawing Room, and slightly earlier overmantel bearing the arms of Elizabeth I, the Long Gallery appears to have survived relatively untouched from the rebuilding of Lyme by Sir Piers VII and his grandson, Sir Peter IX. In fact, however, it has undergone numerous changes in its 400-year history.

The convincingly Jacobean strapwork on the ceiling was executed as recently as 1926, and the panelling has been extensively rearranged. The inner, west wall was probably moved slightly outwards in the early 18th century, the date of the cornice and the fireplace insert. This would have coincided with the introduction of sashes

(Above) The Long Gallery

and the refitting of 'Ye 5 Great Gallery Roomes' adjoining, for the plastering of which a payment was made in June 1732. The panelling was painted white at the same time, and remained so until the room was again altered, by Wyatt, in the early 19th century. A deep bay opposite the fireplace was done away with to allow for a more convenient bedroom corridor running parallel with the Gallery, and the near, south end of the room was opened up, by incorporating what had previously been a peculiarly long and thin bedroom lit by a slanted window. A billiard-table was set up here, and the stage constructed at Christmas for amateur theatricals.

PICTURES

IN FIREPLACE BAY AT NEAR END, FROM LEFT:

ENGLISH, *c.*1630–40
? Rev. Dr Thomas Legh (1594–1639)
Possibly the third son of Sir Peter IX and father of Richard Legh. He was rector of Sefton and Walton in Lancashire.

ENGLISH, *c.*1603
Thomas Egerton, 1st Viscount Brackley (1540?–1617)
Cousin of Dorothy Egerton, second wife of Sir Peter IX. He was Lord Keeper of the Privy Seal in 1596 and 1603 – hence the crimson purse associated with that office.

ENGLISH, *c.*1630–40
Francis Legh (1590–1643)
Second son of Sir Peter IX. He inherited Lyme on the death of his nephew, Peter XI, in February 1642, and died exactly a year later.

ENGLISH, 1631
Sir Peter Legh IX (1563–1636)
Painted when he was 68. For biography, see p. 10. There is a version of this portrait, in stained glass, in the Drawing Room, dated 1634 (illustrated on the back cover).

ENGLISH, 1591
Peter Legh IX (1563–1636)
Painted when he was 28.

ENGLISH, c.1600–10
? *Piers Legh X* (1587/8–1624)
The eldest son of Sir Peter IX, he was disinherited for marrying without his father's consent.

ALONG THE GALLERY, ABOVE THE PANELLING:

On the left is a series of portraits of late 17th-century worthies, on loan from the National Portrait Gallery. Opposite, between the windows, are portraits of members of the family of Rev. Legh Richmond, including his grandmother, Francisca Posthuma, the youngest sister of Richard Legh and wife of Sir Richard Brooke, 2nd Bt. Between the last window and the bay is Richard Legh's second daughter Elizabeth, wife of Sir Streynsham Master.

FURNITURE

Two modern sofas are provided for visitors to rest or to read any of the articles on the house laid out on the table in the southern window bay.

In 1687 the Long Gallery contained just 18 pictures, 24 chairs, a 'Fire Iron' and 'handirons'. By 1879, it had become in part a store for outmoded or broken furniture and worn furnishings. Although cleared at Christmas for the festivities, it did not come back into full use until after the First World War, when Helen Legh (later Lady Newton) gathered together some of the best of the oak furniture and laid out the Long Gallery as an informal drawing-room.

In the Second World War the room was used as a dormitory for the children evacuated to Lyme, and in 1946 much of the oak furniture was sold. The Long Gallery is now furnished with items on loan from the Lady Lever Art Gallery and some important indigenous pieces.

Set of seven walnut side-chairs upholstered in fringed maroon velvet, c.1690.

Set of five Dutch walnut side-chairs, the seats upholstered in silk and velvet floral damask, c.1680, much restored. Original to Lyme.

Oak chest-on-stand, c.1675. On loan from the V&A.

Flemish oak and marquetry chest, c.1610. Possibly made up from other pieces of furniture.

Chinese coromandel-lacquer cabinet, c.1720, on an English giltwood stand with grey-veined marble top, c.1675. Original to Lyme.

Japanese copper-mounted black and gilt-lacquer cabinet, c.1650, on an English silvered stand, c.1680.

English parcel-gilt and olive lacquer bureau decorated with Chinoiserie scenes, c.1705, on a later chest.

Lady Newton performing amateur theatricals with family and friends in the Long Gallery in 1904

English black and gilt lacquer bureau-cabinet, c.1710.

Late 18th-century mahogany bureau bookcase containing a *pair of Paris plates, c.*1800, painted with views of Lyme Park and Hooton Hall, Cheshire, a *'Pearlware' election mug* inscribed 'Peter Legh Esq. Lyme now and forever more. 1789', a mastiff collar and some 18th-century Chinese ceramics.

CLOCK

Eight-day longcase clock in a burr walnut case by John Pashler, London, *c.*1780.

THE TOP CORRIDOR (EAST)

A number of views of Lyme and its interiors are displayed here, including an Augustus Hare watercolour of the portrait of the Black Prince, mid-19th-century watercolours of the Long Gallery and Stag Parlour, a romanticised view of the Drawing Room from Nash's *Mansions of England in the Olden Time* (1849), a watercolour of the house from the west drive, *c.*1870, and a mid-18th-century print after a painting by Francis Smith of stags being driven through the Stag Pond.

Look through the third doorway on the right.

THE OAK BEDROOM

One of four bedrooms along this corridor used in the 19th and early 20th centuries by visiting bachelors. The impressive plaster overmantel of *c.*1600 shows the arms of Sir Richard Hoghton, 1st Bt, of Hoghton Tower in Lancashire, the brother-in-law of Sir Peter IX. Sir Peter was so proud of his marriage to the daughter of Sir Gilbert Gerard – Elizabeth I's Attorney-General and Master of the Rolls – that he commissioned elaborate over-mantels commemorating not only her parents, but also the husbands of her two sisters. All three may originally have been in the north range, which, until the early 18th century, seems always to have held the principal rooms of the house.

Return along the East Corridor and turn left.

THE KNIGHT'S BEDROOM

Also known as the Ghost's Room because it is said to be haunted. A skeleton is reputed to have been found in the large void which exists under the floor, and a supposed priest's hole, entered from the cupboard in the south-west corner, was said to lead, via a secret tunnel, to the Cage. Despite such disturbing tales and the contortions of its furniture and architecture, the room, which was normally reserved for fearless bachelors, was favoured by the widowed mother of Evelyn, Lady Newton. She was not, according to Phyllis Sandeman, afraid of the supernatural but did have an obsessional fear of burglars and considered herself as safe as she could be from them at this high level.

FIREPLACE

The stone fireplace with its plaster overmantel of *c.*1600 was probably moved here from elsewhere in the house in the early 18th century. The arms, of Gerard impaling Radcliffe, are those of the parents of Margaret Gerard, Sir Peter IX's first wife.

The Knight's Bedroom

CEILING

The strapwork ceiling is early 17th-century and provided the model for that in the Long Gallery. It was cut off opposite the window when Wyatt inserted the East Corridor.

BED

The four-poster bed is a typically exuberant early 19th-century revival piece in the Elizabethan style, incorporating 16th-century elements.

THE KNIGHT'S DRESSING ROOM

The hotch-potch of panelling in this room must have been introduced by Lewis Wyatt in 1814–18. It is all late 16th- or early 17th-century and includes sections from the old Stag Parlour as well as a bulbous carving over the fireplace, in a strapwork surround and painted with the ram's head of the Leghs. The fireplace itself is early 18th-century with a 19th-century iron grate.

THE TOP CORRIDOR (NORTH)

This, again, is made up of fragments of reused panelling, some of it late 17th-century. It was a service corridor, and the other rooms off it were used in the 19th century by visitors' valets and footmen.

TURRET CLOCK

By William Leigh of Newton in Lancashire and dated 1814. There has been a turret clock at Lyme since at least the late 17th century; the current one was installed as part of the restoration carried out by Wyatt. The clock strikes the hour but only the sound of the mechanism can be heard from inside, the ceiling beneath the bell being well insulated. The great pendulum swings in the mezzanine void above the Yellow Dressing Room, and the clock weights descend to the side of the north entrance arch beneath that, being deflected by a series of pulleys.

THE NORTH STAIRS

There are three service stairs at Lyme, this one probably dating from the 1730s. It was used by menservants only in the 19th century, when the sexes were rigorously segregated. Above the quarter landing is a full-length portrait of *Colonel Thomas Peter Legh* (1753–97) by James Cranke the Younger. Colonel Legh was the nephew and successor of Peter XIII. He is chiefly remembered for siring seven illegitimate children and, in 1794, raising six troops of cavalry in fourteen days.

The first-floor landing is dominated by the recently conserved painting of *The Derby Stag*, possibly another work of the mid-17th-century monogrammist J.H. (see pp.24 and 26). It is the earliest representation of the famed Lyme Red deer. According to family tradition the animal depicted is that hunted by the Earl of Derby, hence its name.

Off the landing is one of Lyme's early 20th-century bathrooms, with distinctive green and white tiles and a weighty cast-iron bath. The space had previously been a closet to the Tapestry Dressing Room and in 1687 it contained a 'Canopie Bed with Silk Curtains' and a chair. The window has been blocked since the construction of the Bright Gallery in the early 18th century.

THE TAPESTRY DRESSING ROOM

This room was refitted by Richard Legh for the visit of the Duke of York (later James II) in July 1676. It forms the closet, or most intimate space, of the suite of three rooms which served as the state apartments until Leoni's south range was finished in the 1730s. In the early 19th century they were restored by Wyatt for Thomas Legh's own use, but regained their former status after the succession in 1857 of the 1st Lord Newton, and were prepared for the visit of the Crown Prince of Sweden in 1879.

Following conservation the room is entirely hung with tapestries. On the window and fireplace walls are the two earliest in the collection, sadly cut to fit their positions. They are early to mid-16th-century in date, entirely woven from wool and of either English or Flemish manufacture. The other two tapestries are Flemish, that depicting boys bathing being late 17th-century and the verdure showing the sacrifice of a bear, early 17th-century.

THE YELLOW BEDROOM

Richard Legh wrote to his wife from London in 1675: 'I have been to look at some Marble Chimneypieces.... I find there is a White Marble veyn'd and a delicate reddish marble full of white and color'd streakes. These are the two colours I intend to fix upon.' The reddish marble chimneypiece was destined for this room and the white one for the Morning Room next door. The following year, sash-windows were put in, but Richard Legh rejected the marble sills recommended by the stone mason. According to Sir Thomas Chicheley, whose advice he always took on such matters, they were apt to 'perpetually cast a moysture, if you lay but a paire of Gloves down they will be wett'.

Although the Yellow Bedroom, with its plain cornice and simple plasterwork, is now comparatively austere, traces of a fine flock wallpaper, claret-coloured with embossed flowers in green

An English settee, c.1690, upholstered with possibly French silk-embroidered wool, in the Yellow Bedroom

and black, have been found in the adjoining closet or wig cupboard. The effect of this paper and the 'flowered Velvett Bedd ... with ... four white feathers on the topp' listed in the 1687 inventory must have been very sumptuous indeed.

PICTURES

OVER FIREPLACE:

Studio of Sir PETER LELY (1618–80)
Catherine Sedley, Countess of Dorchester (d. 1717)
Mistress of James II.

OVER DOORS:

Manner of Sir GODFREY KNELLER, Bt
(1646/9–1723)
Frances Legh, Mrs Legh (1670–1728)
Wife of Peter XII and daughter and heiress of Piers Legh of Bruch. Dated 1696.

Manner of MICHAEL DAHL (1656–1743)
Frances Legh, Mrs Legh (1670–1728)

TAPESTRIES

Three verdure tapestries with animals: *Ostrich with Dog and Foxes*; *Horse attacked by Leopard*; *Lion and Cock*. Flemish, early 17th-century, probably after 17th-century cartoons.

FURNITURE

The room contains some of the finest 17th-century furniture in the house.

State bedstead, c.1700. Re-upholstered in yellow silk with deep tasselled fringing in the early 19th century and again, in pale yellow silk and wool, in the 1970s.

English settee with grained frame, c.1690, upholstered with contemporary, possibly French, silk-embroidered wool. An early upholstered settee and a rare survival. The seat cushions are of different sizes, one probably intended for a matching stool.

English blue-japanned table and pair of candlestands, c.1680, possibly decorated by Elizabeth Legh, whose sister, Sarah Fountaine, sent a small quantity of varnish 'for a Tryall' in 1681. In 1684 Mrs Legh wrote to her husband, Richard: 'I would desire thee to rit out the receet [recipe] of Japanning for Sa. Bankes' (her sister-in-law). The set was split up and sold in 1945, and returned from the US in 1992.

The Yellow Bedroom in 1900

Pair of English high-backed side-chairs with ebonised frames, the seats upholstered in 19th-century pink and gold brocade with elaborate original fringing, *c*.1685.

Grained pier-table with black and yellow marble top, *c*.1750, and *giltwood pier-glass*, *c*.1710.

Portuguese brass-mounted fruitwood and seaweed marquetry strongbox, *c*.1650, on a similarly decorated English chest, *c*.1690. Original to Lyme.

THE MORNING ROOM

The Morning Room is the last and most public of the late 17th-century state apartments and is listed in the 1687 inventory as 'the Withdrawing Room'. It would have served as an ante-room or sitting-room in which the distinguished occupant of the Yellow Bedroom could receive guests or from where they would be ushered through to either the bedroom or the dressing-room, depending upon their status. In 1687 the Morning Room was as

richly furnished as the Yellow Bedroom, having twelve carved walnut chairs, twelve blue damask cushions, tapestries and 'a blue Jar'. The contents of the whole suite were valued at £500 – one-eighth of the combined total for Lyme and Haydock Lodge in Lancashire.

PICTURES

JOHN MICHAEL WRIGHT (1617–94)
Francisca Posthuma Legh, Lady Brooke (b.1639/40)
Painted when she was 43. She was the youngest, and, as her name suggests, posthumous, daughter of the Rev. Dr Thomas Legh. She married, in 1656, Sir Richard Brooke, 2nd Bt, of Norton Priory. Her third daughter, Frances, married Silvester Richmond (see p.29).

ENGLISH, late 17th-century
? *Sir Richard Brooke, 2nd Bt* (d.1709)
The husband of Francisca Posthuma Legh was High Sheriff of Cheshire in 1667.

TAPESTRIES

The tapestries may still be in the late 17th-century arrangement (apart from that on the inner wall), or have been hung like this *c*.1814, when Wyatt introduced the fine four-flock wallpaper, in a design similar to those of the heraldic artist Thomas Willement.

ON EAST AND WEST WALLS:

Three landscapes with small figures in thistle borders: *Woman with casket of jewels*; *Man playing a Flute*; *Three Pastoral Figures*. English or Brussels, *c*.1670.

ON SOUTH WALL:

The Continence of Scipio
Brussels, *c*.1665, after designs by Giulio Romano (1499–1546). The only tapestry at Lyme with metal thread other than the Mortlakes, it would have looked particularly sumptuous when first acquired. The Roman general Scipio, in a legendary act of clemency, restores unharmed a captured woman to her betrothed.

FURNITURE

Pair of English high-backed armchairs with ebonised frames, the seats upholstered in pink and gold brocade with elaborate fringing, *c*.1685. *En suite* with the side-chairs in the Yellow Bedroom.

(Above) Woman with casket of jewels; one of the 17th-century Flemish tapestries in the Morning Room

Two from a set of seven English side- and armchairs, upholstered in red, green and blue floral crewel-work on linen, *c.*1760.

*English walnut secretaire, c.*1700.

English walnut side-table with oyster-veneered top and barleytwist legs, *c.*1695.

English satinwood card-table, early 19th-century.

THE BRIGHT GALLERY

Creating a gallery at first-floor level round three sides of the courtyard was one of Leoni's most successful achievements at Lyme. Before then, the west range could only be reached from the Entrance Hall by walking through the state apartments on the north or south sides. The Bright Gallery, so-called because of the light from its many windows, was constructed under the direction of John Moore, who, in 1735, was paid for 'two Dorrick Door Cases and Doors (one of them fixed up into my M^r.'s Bed Chamber and the other not yet sett up)'. The doorway at the northern end of the central corridor probably led into Peter XII's rooms, that at the southern end into the 18th-century state rooms. A third arched doorway, without the Doric surround of the other two, leads to the Oak and Acorn Rooms.

DECORATION

The gallery was redecorated in 1998, in the late 19th-century scheme of bright red with grained joinery, window reveals and cornice. It thus matches the Grand Staircase, the two spaces having always, historically, been decorated as one.

PICTURES

CENTRAL SECTION:

ENGLISH, early 18th-century
A member of the Hanbury Family

JOHN ASTLEY (*c*.1730–87)
Four portraits by the Cheshire artist and bon viveur of *the Rev. Legh Richmond* (d.1769), his wife *Mary Legh* and his daughters *Anne* and *Frances Richmond.* Mr Richmond and his wife were both descended from Richard Legh. Astley also painted their other two daughters, Letitia and Mary (see p.29).

ENGLISH, *c*.1650
John Hewitt, D.D. (1614–58)
A Royalist martyr, the lengthy inscription on the painting records his biography. He wears the scarlet robes of a Doctor of Divinity. The picture was sold from Lyme in 1946 and re-acquired in 2001.

SOUTH SECTION:

UNKNOWN ARTIST
*A View of Lyme Hall from the North, c.*1700
This picture was returned to Lyme in 1999 with the help of the National Art Collections Fund and the East Cheshire Association of the National Trust, and depicts the house before the early 18th-century alterations. To the left of the frontispiece on the first floor, you can see the sash-windows introduced by Richard Legh in 1676, some of the earliest in the country. Bowls are being played on the terrace.

FLEMISH SCHOOL, 17th-century
River Landscape with Figures
From the Knaresborough collection, inherited by Helen, Lady Newton.

SCULPTURE

NORTH SECTION:

Set of four early 19th-century English plaster casts taken from the frieze of the Mausoleum at Halicarnassus (Bödrum in modern Turkey), depicting battle scenes between the Greeks and the Amazons. On loan from Manchester Museum.

CENTRAL SECTION:

Early 19th-century plaster cast in three sections of the frieze of the late 5th century BC from the Temple of Apollo Epicurius at Bassae near Phigaleia in Greece. The upper section depicts the battle between the Lapiths and the Centaurs, the lower that between the Greeks and the Amazons. The small section opposite shows Apollo and Artemis in a chariot drawn by stags. The casts were given to Thomas Legh in recognition of his role in removing the original frieze and securing it for the

The Bright Gallery in 1904

British Museum in 1813. One of his colleagues in this venture was the architect C.R. Cockerell.

ALFRED GATLEY (1816–63)
Thomas Legh (1792–1857), 1844
Gatley was from an old Cheshire family and undertook numerous commissions for the Leghs, including Thomas Legh's memorial tablet in Disley church.

ALFRED GATLEY (1816–63)
Maud Lowther, Mrs Legh, 1844
The daughter of Gorges Lowther, of Hampton Hall, Somerset, and the second wife of Thomas Legh, whom she married in 1843.

*Italian marble reduction of the Warwick vase, c.*1830.

FURNITURE

NORTH SECTION:

English giltwood side-table with *verde antico* marble top, c.1760.

Four from a set of six English mahogany side-chairs on acanthus-carved cabriole legs, c.1750, upholstered in pink floral damask.

Three English walnut chests-on-stands, two of c.1700 and one of c.1690. The latter was removed from Lyme in 1946 but recently returned to the house by a member of the family.

Pair of English walnut side-chairs with cane-filled back-splats and caned seats, c.1690.

CENTRAL SECTION:

*Three English walnut chests-on-stands, c.*1690, 1720 or later and c.1690.

*English walnut escritoire-on-stand, c.*1700.

*Set of four Venetian carved side-chairs, c.*1690.

SOUTH SECTION:

Two English walnut chests, one of c.1690 and the other, with oyster veneer, of c.1700.

METALWORK

*Pair of giltmetal colza oil lamps, c.*1820, fitted for electricity c.1903.

CERAMICS

ON SIDE-TABLE AND CHESTS:

Chinese blue-and-white vase with cover, Xianlong, early 18th-century.

*Chinese export ware tureen and cover, c.*1800.

Pair of Chinese blue-and-white beaker vases, Kangxi, c.1662–1722.

Pair of Chinese 'Gu'-shaped famille verte beaker vases, Kangxi, c.1662–1722.

Large Chinese blue-and-white bowl, late 19th-century.

IN DISPLAY CUPBOARDS, CENTRAL SECTION:

Collection of Greek pottery vases and figures, 6th–3rd centuries BC on loan from Manchester Museum.

Collection of 18th- and early 19th-century glass including six Jacobite toasting glasses, c.1740, and six cut-glass, double-lipped wine-glass coolers, c.1815.

Take the central door off the Bright Gallery

THE OAK AND ACORN DRESSING ROOM AND BATHROOM

The dressing-room is on the central axis of the house and has the same architectural details as the Bright Gallery. It was probably intended to serve as an adjunct to the gallery as well as being a dressing-room to one of the principal bedchambers of the house. The former closet of this suite of rooms had been converted into a bathroom and lavatory by 1908.

PICTURES

On the fireplace wall are two portraits of *The Hon. Phyllis Legh, Mrs Gerard Sandeman* (1895–1986), the larger by Frederic Whiting and the smaller by L. Daviel. Mrs Sandeman, the third daughter of the 2nd Lord Newton, was passionately fond of her childhood home and was the author and illustrator of *Treasure on Earth* (1952), a disguised description of Christmas at Lyme in 1906. Her own painting, *Servants' Ball at Lyme Park, circa* 1908, records the annual New Year's Eve event at which Lord and Lady Newton would start the dancing with the housekeeper and butler. Over the door to the bathroom is a portrait of *Francis Legh,* sixth son of Richard Legh, painted in 1732. Opposite is *Dr Calverley Legh* (1682–1727), fourth son of Richard Legh, and *Piers Frederick Legh,* brother of the 1st Lord Newton, both by unknown English artists.

FURNITURE

Early 19th-century mahogany glazed bookcase containing pieces from two late 19th-century tea services, one of them from the Worcester factory, the other ordered as part of the wedding trousseau of the Hon. Mabel Legh, Lady Langford.

A pair of high-back walnut side-chairs, c.1690.

THE OAK AND ACORN BEDROOM

Lyme was amongst the great houses of England that opened their doors to visitors in the mid-19th century and this was one of the principal bedrooms off the Bright Gallery shown, along with the State, Mahogany (not open now) and Yellow Bedrooms. Family bedrooms were not at that time opened.

When James Lees-Milne of the National Trust came to discuss the future of Lyme with the 3rd Lord Newton in November 1943, it was in this room that he stayed, managing to extinguish almost all the lights in the house by plugging in an electric bed-warmer he had brought with him to combat the intense cold of the house.

The high status of the room is indicated by the fact that in the late 17th century it was fully panelled and from the mid-18th century it was hung with an expensive crimson-flock wallpaper, substantial fragments of which were discovered during restoration work in 2002–3. It is now hung with a reprint of a mid-19th-century Persian-tile pattern paper, following the type of redecoration done here and elsewhere in the house by Thomas Legh, probably after his second marriage in 1843. Up to then the room was known as the Velvet Bedchamber, its flock wallpaper being intended to appear as if cut velvet and its bed, which could have been that recorded in what is now the Yellow Bedroom in 1687, probably having crimson velvet hangings. The recent restoration was made possible by a grant from the Wolfson Foundation.

FIREPLACE

The mid-18th-century white marble surround with specimen inserts was probably installed by Peter Legh XIII as part of his finishing of the interiors of Lyme following Leoni's structural alterations for his uncle, Peter XII.

BED

The hangings of the half-tester bed date from about 1700 and, although not indigenous to Lyme, are comparable to what was probably in this room up to the mid-19th century. They are highly important in their own right, being possibly the only survivals of the immensely rich textile hangings acquired for Kimbolton Castle in Huntingdonshire by the 1st Duke of Manchester, many of them from Italy whilst he was Ambassador to the Venetian Republic. The crimson silk-velvet and the exquisitely embroidered cream silk are remnants from the wall panels and bed in the room sumptuously prepared for an anticipated visit of King William III. The trimmings to the curtains and valance of the bed, which incorporate silver-gilt thread, are early 18th-century and come from another room at Kimbolton, probably Vanbrugh's State Bedroom. The velvet and trimmings must have been put together at some time after 1911, when the hangings in King William's Bedroom were last recorded in situ. The window valance is a combination of mid-19th-century green velvet with an 'antiqued' finish and a red-silk knotted fringe of *c.*1700. Originally considerably longer, it was in the Green Drawing Room at Kimbolton. The hangings were donated to the National Trust in the mid-1990s and allocated to Lyme because of the important 17th- and 18th-century furnishing textiles already in the collection.

PICTURES

To the right of the bed is a 19th-century British portrait, possibly of *William Legh* (d. 1834), father of the 1st Lord Newton. Over the adjoining doorway is *A lady of the Turner family*, by Henry Wyatt, *c.*1837, lent by the Lancashire County Museum Service and Higher Mill Museum Trust. Previously thought to be of Ellen Turner, first wife of Thomas Legh, the age of the sitter and the date of her costume make this impossible. Opposite the windows are a copy of Titian's *Danae with Cupid* and *Emily Wodehouse, Lady Newton* by an unknown mid-19th-century British artist. On the fireplace wall are two oval chalk drawings by J.B. Swinton of the *1st Lord and Lady Newton* flanking John Singer Sargent's portrait of *Ethel Pottinger, Lady Knaresborough* (1866–1922), mother-in-law of the 3rd Lord Newton. Lord Newton's mother, Evelyn Bromley Davenport, was the first Englishwoman to be painted by Sargent, and up to 1946 her portrait was also in this room.

FURNITURE

The giltwood pier-glass of *c.*1720 is original to Lyme as is the *walnut bureau* of *c.*1710. The *walnut settee* upholstered in contemporary tapestry is of *c.*1720 and the mahogany and satinwood card-table of *c.*1795.

Return to the Bright Gallery and proceed to the far end.

THE STATE BEDROOM AND DRESSING ROOM
(CLOCK ROOMS)

These rooms were fitted out as the State Bedroom and Dressing Room in the early 18th century. Five panels of Mortlake tapestry were hung on the walls and a state bed was bought by Peter XII at the sale of William, 1st Earl Cadogan's effects in 1727. Peter XII was particularly pleased with the bed, which was upholstered in red Venetian silk: 'one of the finest I have seen, very noble and as fine as any in England.' By 1879 only fragments survived, in store with the tapestries in the Long Gallery.

The rooms were used by the 1st Lord and Lady Newton as their bedroom and dressing-room in the late 19th century, and in the same way by the 3rd Lord and Lady Newton until their departure in 1946. They now contain a display of 18th-century furnishing textiles and the important collection of English clocks acquired and bequeathed by the 3rd Lord Newton's youngest son, Major the Hon. Sir Francis Legh. Sir Francis's collection of clocks was augmented in 2007 by a loan from Mr M.H. Vivian.

PICTURES

DRESSING ROOM:

Opposite the windows are portraits by a late 17th-century English artist of *Peter Vansittart* (1651–1705) and his wife *Susanna Sanderson* (d. 1725), the parents of Robert and Arthur Vansittart (see p. 24). The portrait over the fireplace is of *Charles I*.

BEDROOM:

Over the fireplace is *Charles II* by an unknown artist. Over the doors are two 18th-century portraits by unknown artists of a member of the Hanbury-Williams family and Thomas Winnington, Paymaster General to the Forces in 1743. To the left of the exit door is *George II* from the studio of Charles Jervas.

(Right) An eight-day musical clock, by John Berry, London, c.1735 (Entrance Hall). From Sir Francis Legh's famous clock collection, which is displayed throughout the house

TEXTILES

BEDROOM:

In the display case opposite the fireplace is an ornamented headboard (recently conserved) which survives from the state bed acquired for the room in 1727. The ravages of time and, in particular, light are clear but the sophisticated and delicate design can still be appreciated. In stark contrast are the chair covers opposite the windows – these also date from the 18th century but were never used and, being protected from light, have retained their remarkably strident original colours.

CLOCKS

The Sir Francis Legh collection illustrates the development of English clocks from the 1650s, when the first pendulum mechanisms were developed, to the end of the 18th century, by which time there had been numerous advances in accuracy, control and complexity of striking. During this period clocks also developed as pieces of furniture, reaching great heights of sophistication by the mid-18th century. There are examples by the pre-eminent clockmakers of the period: Joseph Knibb (1640–1711), Thomas Tompion (1639–1713) – considered by some to be the greatest of all clockmakers – and George Graham (1674–1751). Amongst the Tompions is an important group of five collected by Hugh Vivian, on loan from his son from 2007. Sir Francis Legh's automata clocks are displayed throughout the house.

Return to the Bright Gallery and descend by the Brown or Housekeeper's Stairs to the Courtyard. To your right are the doors to the Housekeeper's Room (Shop) and the Stone Parlour.

STONE PARLOUR
(TICKET OFFICE)

This was the upper servants' sitting-room and contains the most magnificent of the three armorial overmantels commissioned by Sir Peter Legh IX to commemorate his prestigious first marriage. The arms are those of Molyneux for one of his wife's brothers-in-law. Hares are depicted amongst grass in the plasterwork and are an unusual motif as well as being of particular charm. The fireplace was

moved here from elsewhere in the house, probably in the late 17th century. The 17th-century buffet niche may be that removed by Wyatt from the Drawing Room in about 1818.

Cross the Courtyard diagonally and take the corridor which leads past the Servants' Hall (not normally open) to the Chapel.

THE CHAPEL

There has probably been a chapel in this space since the late 16th or early 17th century, but the earliest elements now visible – the frieze of cherubs in the sanctuary, the altar rail and the pearwood carvings of the family pew – were introduced by Richard Legh, *c.*1680, when the bay containing the sanctuary was rebuilt. John Moore was being paid for carpentry-work here in the 1730s and created a new staircase to give access to the family pew from the Entrance Hall. He must also have introduced the screen of fluted Ionic pillars.

In the early 19th century there were collegiate stalls in the main body of the Chapel and an octagonal pulpit. Wyatt was probably responsible for a short-lived central pulpit, of which there is evidence in the floor, and for placing Gothic tracery in front of the 18th-century sashes. His were the last significant alterations, apart from the removal of the pews.

After 1900 the Chapel was rarely used. According to Phyllis Sandeman, it became 'a storing place for surplus furniture, chairs and rout seats for dances and Fraulein's [the governess's] bicycle'. Lady Newton is said to have regretted this, being consoled only by the fact that 'because of being under the drawing room it was not consecrated'. The Chapel has been in use again since 1950, when it was reconsecrated and the present pulpit was installed.

In the Ante-Chapel are part of a Saxon cross and a stoup, both of which were dug up on the estate in the 19th century.

THE GARDEN AND PARK

HISTORY OF THE GARDEN

At 240 metres above sea level, with a short growing season and an average of 100 cm of rainfall per year, Lyme is an unlikely place for a garden. Yet gardening has been going on here to good effect for at least 400 years. Successive generations of the family created a lush and colourful oasis on this unusual site, carved out of a hillside beneath the once heather- and holly-clad moorland, despite no doubt agreeing with Richard Legh's head gardener, who complained in 1683 of 'what a strange, cold place itt is and he cannot have things soe early as his neighbours'.

It was probably Sir Peter Legh IX who laid the foundations of the garden, payments being recorded in 1609 for arbours and 'Quicksetts for the new poole', but the first visual records are late 17th-century paintings of the house from the north, which show the garden created by Richard Legh in the 1670s and 1680s: walled and tree-lined enclosures to the north and west, a formal grass parterre with a central fountain to the side of the north forecourt, and urn-topped terraces with gazebos to the east, reached by a bridge from the first-floor Great Dining Room (now the Drawing Room). The main surviving feature shown is the lime avenue, which aligns with the centre of the south front. The fragmentary painting at the head of the Grand Staircase hints at the formal piece of water to the south of the house, to which Sir John Chicheley referred in 1676: 'The alteration yo intend about yr Pond must needs be pleasant, and of some use for diversion wch now is none: yo must take care yr Statue be proportonable to ye Bignesse of Yr Pond otherwise twill show not well. …'

The pond was further worked upon for Peter Legh XII in 1734, when Peter Platt was paid for 'Getting and working stone used in the pedestall on the Island upon the Great Pond'. The cascade created about 1700, probably in emulation of that at Chatsworth, was altered at the same time, and a hanging garden laid out on the surrounding slopes. Both were swept away in 1814–18 by Lewis Wyatt, who also naturalised the pond, laid out the North Garden and began building the orangery. It was left to the 1st Lord Newton, following his succession in 1857, to finish the orangery and to exploit the dramatic opportunities presented by the terraces to the east and the great buttressed walls to the west. Lord Newton was advised by the garden writer and theorist Edward Kemp, and, following his *How to lay out a Garden* (1850), formal bedding was introduced: both in sunken beds on the orangery terrace, where the natural incline allowed it to be viewed from a number of vantage points; and, in the form of an Italianate parterre, on the site of the 18th-century hanging garden. The parterre (later, following fashion, renamed the Dutch Garden) was intended to be viewed from above, either from the garden walks or the west drive. Following Kemp's principles, the Dutch Garden divides the polished surroundings of the house from the picturesque park beyond, where nature reigns.

The 2nd Lord Newton, as his daughter Phyllis Sandeman recalled, 'preferred to people the glades of his water garden with exotic birds'. His wife laid out flower borders to the east of the terraces and an intimate rose garden beside the orangery. Standards continued to be maintained after the First World War by the future 3rd Lady Newton, whose meticulousness earned her the respect of many of the gardeners and the fear of others. She developed the herbaceous borders from the narrow Edwardian flower-beds laid out by her mother-in-law. The ravine known as 'Killtime', which had formed a wilderness walk since at least the early 18th century, was filled with lush planting to bring it properly into the garden.

Lyme House in Cheshire

(Above) The north front around 1700 (Bright Gallery)

The garden was inevitably neglected during the Second World War, but since 1946 its structures, sculpture and plantings have slowly been restored to their early 20th-century zenith. This has been achieved by the head gardener and his team of gardeners, and has been assisted by donations from the National Gardens Scheme, National Trust members' associations, the Ironmongers' Company and the late Mrs Denise Leffman.

TOUR OF THE GARDEN

The tour follows an anti-clockwise route starting from the west terrace, which is reached by turning right out of the south entrance.

The west terrace was created by Wyatt in about 1814 as part of his buttressing of the south-west corner of the house. With its corner-bastions and low, enclosing railings, it is designed to command views over the Dutch Garden to the park beyond and, back across the south lawn and lake, to the starkly contrasting Park Moor. Urns, then of cast iron, were first introduced in the mid-19th century,

and the low yew hedges were planted at the turn of the last century.

The sweep of lawn before the south front runs down to the lake which reached its current form in the mid-19th century. The pump-house beside it was built in 1902 to provide water in case of fire. On the island are planted the deciduous azalea and *Rhododendron campanulatum*, and, on the far bank, a Western Hemlock (*Tsuga heterophylla*) from the western United States, planted by the 4th Lord Newton in 1936, on his 21st birthday.

From the path alongside the south lawn, and a parallel path below, the visitor can look across steep banks clothed with shrubs to the intricate Dutch Garden. Laid out by the 1st Lord Newton in the 1860s, the parterre surrounding the fountain-pool is a pattern of grass paths with beds edged by box and ivy and is planted with traditional spring and summer bedding schemes in the 19th-century manner. The statues represent the four elements – Earth, Air, Fire and Water – and are replacements of the lead originals, sold in 1945.

The lower path is reached from opposite the pump-house and leads to an area beyond the Dutch Garden, which, until the mid-19th century, was the drying ground for the laundry. It is now known as the Vicary Gibbs garden, after a friend of the family, who was, according to Phyllis Sandeman, 'given *carte blanche* to come every summer … to lay down the law and to generally interfere'. Gibbs presented trees and shrubs from his famous garden at Aldenham in Hertfordshire, including the Mirbeck's oak (*Quercus canariensis*), Hungarian oak (*Quercus frainetto*), Chinese Cornel (*Cornus kousa*), a hybrid chestnut with reddish flowers, a hybrid red buckeye (*Aesculus × hybrida*), a thorn bush with upright growth (*Crataegus monogyna* 'Stricta'), and a variegated sycamore (*Acer pseudoplatanus* 'Leopoldii'). The area is extensively underplanted with spring bulbs.

Returning to the pump-house and crossing a little oak bridge on the right-hand side, a path leads between the lake and Calves Croft (the fallow deer park), passing the end of the lime avenue, which was replanted in the mid-19th century. The trees at the far end had to be replaced again following storm damage in the 1980s. Beyond the lake the path splits, the right-hand spur leading up a steep incline to the rhododendron walk, which was created in 1985 and passes the site of the 17th-century kitchen garden, which stood to the right, in Calves Croft. Also to the right, in a clearing half-way along, are four small-leaf limes (*Tilia platyphyllos* 'Rubra') planted by the children of the present Lord Newton and the oldest and youngest estate tenants in 1995 to celebrate the centenary of the National Trust. Steps descend to Hampers Bridge, which bears the date 1751 and is thought to have been moved eastwards, probably following the relocation of the kitchen garden in the early 19th century. The numbers on many of the stones may relate to its rebuilding.

The bridge arches over a pond backed by azaleas and marks the start of the deep ravine known as 'Killtime' because of its historic status as the favourite retreat of badgered gardeners. The banks are planted with moisture-loving primulas, astilbes, irises, hostas and ferns with azaleas and other flowering shrubs, whilst in the early summer mauve rhododendrons tumble down from above. Aged oaks, beech and limes tower overhead. Above the north bank is one of Lyme's many quartets of the small-leafed lime, together with a number of conifers. The stream eventually disappears into a culvert, to re-emerge in the lake.

Paths from Killtime lead to the top lawn, at the lower end of which, beneath some ancient yews, is a curious stone table believed to have been

The Dutch Garden

The Orangery Terrace

constructed for cock-fighting. Beyond the top lawn are the 3rd Lady Newton's double herbaceous borders, now laid out to a scheme by Graham Stuart Thomas with a great variety of perennial plants graded according to colour, strongest at the entrance and decreasing to paler shades at the far end. The borders are backed by some good hollies, including *Ilex altaclerensis* 'Hodginsii' with broad, dark leaves, and some white and variegated forms of the common holly.

The rose garden, entered from the terrace below or alternatively along a recently planted yew walk, was created in 1913 on the site of two pit-greenhouses. It was restored in 1995. Formal beds, containing dwarf floribunda roses, are laid out in a symmetrical pattern around a small pond, and there are standard roses at the four corners. Next to the rose garden is Wyatt's orangery, which was completed in 1862 by Alfred Darbyshire. It

contains two massive camellias, probably intro-duced in the 1860s, together with figs, palms and abutilons and is fronted by a terrace guarded by clipped Irish yews. The formal panel beds, in the form of crosses and wheels, yearly receive thousands of annual plants, including, in the summer, the old heliotrope (*Heliotropium* 'Lord Roberts'), and *Penstemon* 'Rubicundus', which was first raised at Lyme in 1906. At the far end of the terrace a stone walkway constructed by Wyatt leads to a bastion or viewing platform from where his North Garden can be appreciated. It was restored in 2001 and is an early example of the 19th-century revival of formality in garden design. The long, or pantry, border below the orangery terrace is planted with perennials according to another scheme by Graham Stuart Thomas, drawn up in 1966. The weeping silver linden (*Tilia* 'Petiolaris') to the left of the path was planted in 1947, replacing one which had been there for 150 years.

The path running parallel to the pantry border

(Above) The Cage

leads back, via a series of steps, to the south entrance and affords a spectacular view past the acutely angled south front with its great portico to the urn-topped terrace wall and the sweep of the west drive through the park.

THE PARK

Lyme lies in a corner of Cheshire which is hard-up against the Pennines and quite unlike the rich, pastoral lowland typical of the county. Its resilient, crystalline gritstone and swelling moorland make it more typical of neighbouring Derbyshire and it was probably its role as a physical barrier on the eastern edge of the Cheshire plain that earned the estate its name – from the Latin word for a frontier, *limes*. Lyme was part of the hunting reserve or 'forest' of Macclesfield, which was held by the Earls of Chester until seized by the Crown in 1237. The deer-park was probably enclosed shortly after the estate was granted to Piers and Margaret Legh in 1398 and was described in 1465 as 'a fair park surrounded with a paling and divers fields contained in the same park with the woods, under-woods, meadows, feedings and pastures thereto belonging'. Though its enclosing fence, or 'ryng pale', of timber was replaced by a stone wall about 1598, it is still essentially a medieval deer-park and has never been subject to extensive landscaping. What alterations there were, were primarily under-taken in the late 17th and early 18th centuries, when the park became prized as much for its orna-mental as for its sporting value. Richard Legh laid out axial avenues of sycamore and lime to the north and south of the house in the 1660s and 1670s and established an impressive vista through the keyhole created by the narrowly planted lime avenue, leading to what appears on two late 17th-century paintings to be a triumphal arch. The remains of a simpler, later building, known as the Stag House, survive on the site. Of the two other distant park buildings recorded in the same paintings, that to the south-west of the house, known as Paddock Cottage, survives and has recently been restored. On certain weekends, there is access to the interior of the building, which was constructed by Sir Peter IX and contains the remains of an early 17th-century plaster overmantel depicting his arms.

Richard Legh's avenues were incorporated in a more thorough revamping of the park carried out in the early 18th century by his son, Peter XII. Peter Legh undertook extensive tree-planting, particularly of lines and clumps of beech of which vestiges survive, and established sight lines to, and between, the various park buildings. The curious structure known as the Lantern with its octagonal central section, square base and pyramidal roof, was erected in 1729, probably in part reusing stone from the house. Placed in the steeply rising woods above the top lawn, it can be seen from a number of vantage points in the park, as well as from the rooms along the east front and from the west drive.

Even more prominently sited is the Cage. A

possibly early 16th-century building was taken down in 1734, and payments were made over the following three years for 'masons work in Rebuilding Lyme Cage', probably to the designs of Leoni. There are three principal internal spaces: a columned basement similar in detail to the south entrance of the house; a plaster-panelled first-floor room much restored by Wyatt; and a service room above, all linked by a spiral staircase in one of the turrets. The Cage was primarily for following the hunt or for banquets, but the name probably also implies that it was employed as a temporary prison for felons and, in particular, poachers. The building has recently been restored.

In 1750 Dr Richard Pococke remarked that 'the great curiosity of this place are the red deer'. They had long been held in high esteem, having been hunted by James, Duke of York during his visit in 1676. William Webb wrote in about 1600 of Lyme's 'large and spacious Park richly stored with Red and Fallow Deer', and 150 years later Dr Pococke witnessed the custom of driving red stags across a pond at mid-summer, 'their horns moving like a wood along the water'. Pococke also names the park keeper, Joseph Watson, who was 102 at the time and 'having been in that office since 1674 has seen five generations hunt in the park'. According to a lengthy obituary written on his death three years later, he had once driven twelve brace of stag from Lyme Park to Windsor forest for a wager of 500 guineas. According to Lady Newton in *House of Lyme*, 'The drinking propensity of this ancient retainer is alluded to in several of the old letters, his excesses being much deplored'.

Lyme was no less well-known for its wild cattle, which roamed the park moor and, with their white coats and red ears, were similar in appearance to the Chillingham breed. They were the largest of the wild park breeds and were probably descended from feral cattle roaming within the forest at the time the park was enclosed. Their numbers deteriorated rapidly in the 19th century, from 20 in 1817 to just four in 1875. Despite attempts to save them by cross-breeding, they had become extinct by 1884. Highland cattle now graze the moorland.

The pond through which the deer were driven each year lay immediately in front of the present stable block and had to be filled in when that building was constructed, to the design of Alfred Darbyshire, in 1863–6. By the mid-1870s Darbyshire had also laid out the kitchen garden beyond the stables, and beyond again he added a pheasantry and the kennels which used to house the famous Lyme mastiffs. This allowed the complex of utilitarian buildings on the slope to the north-west of the house to be cleared away, and a suitably grand and picturesque conclusion to the main approaches from the north and west to be created. In 1904 the 2nd Lord Newton employed Charles Reilly, Professor of Architecture at Liverpool University, to accommodate new workshops, a laundry and an electricity generating plant in an Arts and Crafts group of buildings below the mill-pond. Lord Newton was also responsible for the present main drive, which was planned and built by the Stockport nurseryman James Yates in 1902–3 and superseded the Green and Hawthorn drives, higher up the hill. The clumps of Corsican pine along the main drive are part of Yates's scheme.

The Lantern

THE LEGHS AND LYME

THE MEDIEVAL HUNTING LODGE

At the siege of Caen in July 1346 Sir Thomas Danyers had the good fortune to capture the Comte de Tancarville, Chamberlain of Normandy, for whom he was paid the princely ransom of 10,000 Nobles. Sir Thomas was accompanying Edward III's son, the Black Prince, on a raid into northern France to enforce the King's claim to the French throne. At the Battle of Crécy the following month he performed the deed which resulted in the grant of Lyme to the Leghs over 50 years later. Crécy was to prove the greatest English victory of the Hundred Years War, but during the battle a wave of French knights broke through the heavily outnumbered English lines to the Black Prince, who was unhorsed and in danger of death or capture. Not only was Sir Thomas amongst those who saved the Prince, but he also rescued the royal standard, and it was for 'replanting the Prince's banner at Cressi' in particular that he was awarded £40 a year out of the Royal Manor of Frodsham. The grant was to be made until 'land worth £20 a year in some suitable place' should be provided in exchange.

Sir Thomas returned to Cheshire triumphant, was made sheriff of the county for the second time in 1349 and continued in high favour until 1353, when he was indicted for bribery and theft and lost his office. Amongst the catalogue of charges levelled against him were that he had run a protection racket, stolen fish from his neighbours' ponds, and 'that he feloniously broke into the Lord Earl's treasure house' at Chester Castle and stole the bond which recorded a previous debt to the Black Prince as Earl of Chester. He pleaded guilty to all the charges and was fined, but retained possession of his estate and the royal annuity, and on his death in 1354 he was succeeded in both by his grand-daughter, Margaret.

Margaret Danyers was married and widowed

three times and died at the age of 80 in 1428. Her third husband, Piers Legh I (c.1360–99), came from a family, probably of Norman extraction, which had already been living at High Legh in Cheshire for over two centuries and which proved remark-ably successful at establishing landed branches throughout the county. The loyalty of the first Piers to Richard II earned him a grant of arms in 1397 and the long-awaited exchange of the royal annuity for an appropriate piece of land the following year. On 4 January 1398 the King granted Piers and Margaret Legh 'one piece of land and pasture called Hanley, lying in our Forest of Macclesfield, in the County of Chester, which before this was let to farm for 20 marks a year'. The choice of Hanley, or Lyme Hanley, was almost certainly made by Piers himself, for he had been granted 'the herbage of Hanley' in 1383, and he and his brother John had been appointed bailiffs of the nearby borough of Macclesfield in 1382 by Joanna, Princess of Wales. The land granted was predominantly unproductive moorland, and was probably envisaged as a hunting domain. A house was built here, probably about 1400, but it remained a subsidiary residence, at first to Bradley in Cheshire, which had been inherited from Sir Thomas Danyers, and then to another Bradley, in south Lancashire, which came to the Leghs around 1400 through the marriage of Piers's son, Sir Peter II, to Joan of Haydock.

Piers Legh I was one of the first of Richard II's supporters to suffer after the King's downfall in 1399. By order of the usurping Duke of Lancaster, who became Henry IV, he was executed at Chester on 10 August, as the chronicler Hollinshed relates:

King Richard beying in the Castell of Conway sore discomfited and fearing lest he should not remaine there long in safetie ... sent the Duke of Exeter to talke with the Duke of Lancaster, who in the meane while, had caused one of King Richard's faithful and

The Black Prince, who was rescued by Sir Thomas Danyers at the Battle of Crécy in 1346. Danyers was rewarded with an annuity which was exchanged for the Lyme estate in 1398 by his granddaughter, Margaret, and her husband, Piers Legh I. This early 18th-century portrait is prominently displayed in the Entrance Hall

trustie friends Sir Peers a Legh [he was never in fact knighted], commonly called Perkyn a Lee, [to] loose his head and commanded the same be set up, uppon one of the highest turrets aboute all the citie and so that true and faithful Gentleman, for his stedfast faith and assured loyaltie to his louinge soueraigne, thus lost his life.

His mutilated body was initially interred in the church of the Carmelites at Chester, but was later removed to St Michael's, Macclesfield, where it lies with that of his son, Sir Peter II (died 1422). The loyalty of the father and the military prowess of the son, who was knighted at Agincourt, are commemorated in an inscription, placed in the nearby Legh chapel:

Here Lyeth the body of Perkyn a Legh
That for King Richard the death did die
Betrayed for righteousness
And the bones of Sir Peers his sonne
That with King Henry the fift did wonne
In Paris.

Sir Peter III (1415–78) proved more fortunate in his allegiances than his grandfather, Piers I. He joined the Yorkists at Sandal Castle in 1460 and although they were defeated shortly afterwards at the Battle of Wakefield, where he was knighted, he was also present at the Battle of Towton in March 1461, which confirmed Edward IV's recent assumption of the crown. In May 1461 Sir Peter was appointed Governor of Rhuddlan Castle in Flintshire, and the following year he joined the new king's expedition toward Scotland. He was the first of the Leghs of Lyme to survive into old age, dying peaceably in his own bed at Bradley in 1478.

A remarkable survey of over 300 leaves was drawn up for Sir Peter III in 1465, which describes in detail his extensive estates and his three houses: Bradley, the principal seat, and Norley, both in Lancashire, and Lyme in Cheshire. The manor of Lyme was the smallest of the three, consisting of:

… one fair hall with high chamber, kitchen, bakehouse and brewhouse, with a granary, stable and bailiff's house and a fair park, surrounded with paling and divers fields and hays contained in the same park, with the woods, underwoods, meadows, feedings and pastures thereto belonging, which are worth to the said Peter X^I [£10] a year.

THE TUDOR AND STUART HOUSE

With its enclosed deer-park and comparatively small house, Lyme must still have been little more than a hunting lodge, and it did not begin to gain importance until the early 16th century, during the later years of Sir Peter III's grandson and successor, Sir Piers V (1455–1527). Sir Piers had fought under the Duke of Gloucester in the Scottish campaign of 1482 and had received an annuity of £10 from the Duke after he succeeded to the throne as Richard III. At the Battle of Bosworth in 1485 he adroitly changed sides and was rewarded by Henry VII ten years later, when he was presented with the

Tomb brass of Sir Piers Legh V (1455–1527) from the Legh Chapel in Winwick church, Lancashire

lucrative stewardship of Blackburnshire. In 1511, however, he resigned as steward and shortly thereafter, perhaps on the advice of his brother-in-law, Thomas Savage, Archbishop of York, he retreated to Lyme and entered the priesthood. In all subsequent documents he described himself as 'Sir Piers Legh, Knight and Priest', and a few years before his death in 1527, he founded a chapel at Disley near Lyme, which has since become the parish church and is the resting place of recent generations of the family. Sir Piers dictated in his will that he himself should be buried before the altar in the Trinity or Legh Chapel at Winwick church in Lancashire, his body to be placed so that 'the prest shall alwaies [at] the tyme of consecracon stand even over and upon my harte'. The stone slab placed over his body, and subsequently moved to the east end of the chapel, contains brasses commemorating Sir Piers and his wife Ellen, who had died in 1491. His is the only known English monumental brass to combine the military and the sacred, showing the 'Knight and Priest' in clerical vestments worn over armour, with his sword by his side.

Sir Piers V's son, Peter VI (1479–1541), was the last of the family to be styled 'of Bradley and Lyme', rather than vice versa, and although Bradley Hall was repaired in the early 17th century, it was subsequently abandoned and was largely dismantled in the 1740s. Sir Piers VII (1514–89), Peter VI's son, made the final move to Lyme, but before embarking upon ambitious alterations to the house there, he followed in the martial footsteps of his forebears and took part in the Scottish campaigns of 1544 and 1545, led by the Earl of Hertford (later 1st Duke of Somerset and Protector of England). He was amongst those knighted on 11 May 1544, at the sacking of Leith and Edinburgh, and a week later was entrusted with carrying a letter from Lord Hertford to Henry VIII, which commended him for 'having served in this journey [the campaign] both honestly and willingly'.

The exact extent of Sir Piers VII's work at Lyme is unclear, but he was almost certainly responsible for the frontispiece on the north range, which, stylistically, is of about 1570 and owes a strong debt to old Somerset House, the highly influential creation of Sir Piers's former mentor, Protector

Sir Piers Legh VII (1514–89) (private collection)

Sir Peter IX was a sophisticated courtier and patron of the arts, who, after the stint of soldiering expected of a Legh of Lyme, settled down to a life divided between his estates in Cheshire and Lancashire and his parliamentary duties in London, as one of the MPs for Cheshire. He gained important connections by both his marriages – his first wife, Margaret, being the daughter of Elizabeth I's Attorney General and Master of the Rolls, Sir Gilbert Gerard, and his second wife, Dorothy, the half-sister of Lord Chancellor Ellesmere. He maintained a house in Fulham and entertained at Lyme such figures as Robert Devereux, 3rd Earl of Essex, the son of Elizabeth I's disgraced favourite, who was 'invited to hunt the Stagg' in the summer of 1620. By the early 17th century the deer at Lyme were sufficiently famous for Henry Cavendish to request some in order to populate the 'smale red deare parke' he proposed to make 'near unto my house att Chatsworth'. Lyme's mastiffs were also well-known and for some time had made suitable gifts to friends of the Leghs. In November 1584

Somerset. Sir Piers must also have extended the north range, and he probably substantially rebuilt the east or hall range, including the Great Hall and Great Chamber (now the Entrance Hall and Drawing Room). The Long Gallery, however, which runs the full length of the east range above these rooms, was fitted up, and possibly entirely added, only after his death in 1589, by his grandson, Sir Peter IX (1563–1636). Sir Peter IX completed and extended his grandfather's house, adding the Little, or Stag, Parlour on the east front, closing the quadrangle with the south and west ranges and embellishing the interior with panelling, plasterwork and stained glass produced by some of the finest craftsmen of the day. Sir Peter also began creating a suitable setting for the now impressive mansion, gaining a licence from Elizabeth I to enclose the great park with a continuous stone wall and building two belvederes or banqueting houses, one of which survives. In 1609, according to the steward's accounts, a boathouse and a pigeon house were added, and work was underway in the garden.

Sir Peter Legh IX (1563–1636) (Long Gallery)

Robert Dudley, 1st Earl of Leicester, another of Elizabeth's favourites, wrote to his 'very louinge fren', Sir Piers VII, 'I thanke you very hartile Sʳ. Piers for yor hounde and will requyte you the losse of him with as good a thinge'. In 1604 'a Cupple of Lyme hounds of singular qualities' were chosen to form part of the gift sent by James I to Philip III of Spain at the close of the Anglo-Spanish war.

Despite his many courtly attributes, Sir Peter IX was a man of considerable stubbornness and ferocity, in keeping with the severe countenance shown in the numerous portraits of him at Lyme, and his treatment of his children was sometimes harsh to the point of cruelty. The pathetic entreaties of his eldest son, Piers X (1587/8–1624), in the face of parental intransigence, make painful reading. Sir Peter had promised to allow Piers a free hand in choosing his bride after he ended an unsuitable attachment in 1610, but when he presented the thoroughly respectable Anne Savile two years later, Sir Peter still withheld his consent. For five years, Piers tried to persuade his father to change his mind, as did Sir Peter's brothers- and sisters-in-law and his nephew, John, 1st Earl of Bridgewater, who tried to play on his uncle's well-known sense of honour:

You have ever bene noted firme of your worde and promise, let not your sonne be the first with whom you breake it. Good uncle be content … to use the power of a father to the correction and strayne it not to the confusion of a sonne and eldest sonne and such a one as I dare undertake will be a loving and dutyfull sonne....

Piers himself stated his case eloquently in a letter written in about 1617, although he ended with a desperate plea:

Good Sr, if it lye in your powre, or that you can be resolved anyway to dispense with your contrarietie to me, I beseech you with tears and uppon the knees of my soul to compassionate your distressed sonne and lett your tender and deare love yeeld your consent....

Sir Peter was not to be moved, and when Piers finally wed Anne Saville in late 1617 or early 1618, Sir Peter presumably invoked his threat to become 'a mere stranger to me and myne'.

On Piers's death in 1624, his infant son, Peter XI or 'Little Peter' (1623–42), was taken away from his mother and brought up at Lyme, to which he succeeded in 1636 on Sir Peter IX's death. Before he came of age, however, he quarrelled with the eldest son of a Sir John Browne and was fatally wounded in the subsequent duel. The estate passed briefly to his uncle Francis, and then, in 1643, to the eight-year-old Richard Legh (1634–87), eldest son of Francis's next brother, Thomas.

Richard was, like the rest of his family, a staunch Royalist, but the estate was saved from the ravages of the Civil War by his long minority, and it was sufficiently healthy at the Restoration in 1660 to allow him to carry out extensive improvements to the house and garden thereafter. In 1661 he married Elizabeth Chicheley, and over the next 26 years, until his death in 1687, the couple presided over a happy and bustling household, vividly recorded in the numerous letters which survive from the period. Richard Legh was an intimate of the royal family and it was the impending visit of the Duke of York (later James II) which spurred him into fitting up the state apartments in the north range (the

Morning Room and Yellow Bedroom) in 1675–6. He was advised throughout by his wife's father and brother, Sir Thomas and Sir John Chicheley, delaying a decision on fireplaces 'till my Father[-in law] can see them' and being complimented by Sir John in the spring of 1676 on what had been achieved thus far. It may well have been through the influence of Sir Thomas, whose own house at Wimpole in Cambridgeshire was praised by the gentleman-architect Sir Roger Pratt, that sash-windows, then very much a novelty, were installed to light the refitted rooms. In a letter written in 1676, Richard Legh remarked of the contract:

Wilkins Asketh 4^s per yard for the workmanship of plain wainscot and ... 2^s a foot for shass [sash] windowes, that is 18^s a square yard and he find timber, which you know is noe great matter ....

Two late 17th-century paintings of Lyme show the square-paned sashes, together with Richard's other improvements, including the terraces and gazebos in the garden and the lime avenue stretching away to the south of the house. They also show, jutting out from the east front, the 'new parlour', which he had added in 1680 beyond Sir Peter IX's Little or Stag Parlour (where the Dining Room is now). It was probably for the New Parlour that Sir John Chicheley approached Grinling Gibbons in 1684. In addition to Gibbons's carvings (since moved to the Saloon), Richard adorned the interior of Lyme with new mirrors, clocks, furniture, tapestries, portraits by Sir Peter Lely, and even an example of the recently invented 'device ... to know the weather by', or barometer, which he had acquired from the mathematician Sir Jonas Moore in May 1675.

(Left) Richard Legh (1634–87); by Sir Peter Lely. The portrait hangs in the Dining Room which is on the site of Legh's 'New Parlour'

(Right) Peter Legh XII (1669–1744), who commissioned Leoni to remodel the house; by Sir Godfrey Kneller (private collection)

THE 18TH CENTURY

Peter Legh XII, or 'the Elder' (1669–1744), was to prove an energetic builder like his father, whom he succeeded in 1687, but in the years immediately after he inherited, he was deeply involved in political intrigue. He persistently refused to swear the oath of allegiance to William and Mary, following the overthrow of James II in 1688, and was almost certainly the instigator of the Jacobite 'Cheshire Club', the first of whose clandestine meetings was held in the Stag Parlour at Lyme. In 1694 he was arrested in his dressing-room at Lyme and imprisoned in the Tower for complicity in the 'Lancashire Plot', which sought to restore the exiled King. He was charged with high treason then and two years later, but was acquitted on both occasions, and although a further warrant was issued for his arrest in 1705, prudence led him to avoid openly supporting the Old Pretender in 1715. Instead, he had begun devoting himself to transforming the exterior of Lyme, starting with the north front, which was regularised and refenestrated around 1710. The work was probably done

by John Platt, one of the dynasty of masons who had been involved at Lyme since at least Richard Legh's time, when they had built his New Parlour; they remained prominent in the steward's accounts well into the 1730s.

By 1721, Peter Legh had made contact with the influential Venetian architect Giacomo Leoni, who was patronised by the Tory aristocracy and designed two other great houses in the north-west: Bold Hall near Warrington for Peter Bold (a cousin of Peter XII), and Lathom House near Ormskirk for Sir Thomas Bootle. Leoni advised on the west front of Lyme in May 1725, and although that façade is clearly not competent enough to be entirely his work, he was wholly responsible for the south front and the courtyard, the drawings for which he began to produce that year. Work continued for over ten years, primarily involving the recasing of the old house, but also including the creation of a number of internal spaces – the Entrance Hall, Grand Staircase, Saloon and Bright Gallery.

The decoration of the new interiors seems to have been entrusted to the mason and carver John Moore, who was sent to view 'Gentlemens and Noblemens Houses in Lancashire, Derbyshire, Nottinghamshire, Yorkshire, Warwickshire' in 1732. It shows the first signs of the antiquarianism of the family which was to come fully into bloom in the 19th century. In the Entrance Hall, created out of the Elizabethan Great Hall, pride of place was given to a pair of full-length portraits of Edward III and the Black Prince, set up like altarpieces at either end of the room to pay homage to the family's first royal patrons. The portrait of the Black Prince, which survives, swings out to reveal the squint into the Elizabethan Great Chamber (now the Drawing Room). If this is an early Georgian, rather than a Regency conceit, it shows astonishing respect for the antiquity of the house and could also be interpreted as a statement by the Jacobite Peter Legh that his family was of ancient origin and did not owe its rise to either William of Orange or the Hanoverians.

Peter XIII, or the Younger (1708–92), who succeeded in 1744, probably finished some of his uncle's rooms and certainly bought much of the

Colonel Thomas Peter Legh (1753–97); after James Cranke the Younger (private collection)

exceptionally fine mid-18th-century furniture still in the house, including the wonderful suite of giltwood chandeliers in the Saloon, Library and Drawing Room, the 1762 harpsichord by Hitchcock, also in the Saloon, and the numerous console- and side-tables and side-chairs throughout the house. His early years at Lyme were contented and busy; he had a young family and an apparently happy marriage, he was able greatly to develop the coal interests on his estates, and since 1743 he had been MP for Newton-in-Makerfield, the pocket borough in Lancashire acquired by Richard Legh in 1660 from the Fleetwoods. Following the death of his only surviving son, Benet Legh, in 1756, however, his relationship with his wife, Martha, deteriorated and he became increasingly dominated by his manipulative and unpopular spinster sister, Ann. In the 1760s he handed over management of his business interests to his highly competent steward, Richard Orford, and suffered increasingly from bad health, which probably led him to give up his seat in Parliament in 1776. Three years later, a skit on the leading members of Cheshire society called Lyme 'a house divided against itself'. Peter Legh the Younger was presented as a philandering buffoon, 'a good caricature of a body coachman', led astray by his mistress, Lady Mary West (daughter of the 4th Earl of Stamford), and by his sister, and causing his wife's face to be wrinkled with 'the melancholy furrows of excessive grief'. Martha Legh left her husband in 1783, writing to Peter from Weymouth in July of that year:

The uncomfortable life you must needs be sensible I have led in your Family and the sort of behaviour I have met with there for these many years past gives me every room to think that my absence will be by much the most agreeable to every part of it. I therefore propose to continue in this part of the World some length of time longer, for I wish to spend the latter part of these my days with peace and comfort ....

In fact Martha died at Lyme, in 1787, but whether the couple had become reconciled is not known. Peter Legh the Younger was by that time confined to his bath chair, in which he was wheeled up and down the Bright Gallery, and he himself died in 1792, at the age of 84.

As Peter the Younger's sons both died young, Lyme passed to his nephew, the roguish Colonel Thomas Peter Legh (1753–97). He was best known for having raised six troops of cavalry in fourteen days in 1794 – following Pitt's call to arms in the face of increasing trouble in Europe – and for having sired seven children by seven different women, none of whom was his wife. He was also responsible for the building of a vast new house at Haydock in Lancashire and for denuding Lyme of much of its woodland, presumably to pay for his extravagances. 'Pity it is', wrote an obituarist in the *Gentleman's Magazine* of August 1797, following the Colonel's untimely death that month from a fit of apoplexy, 'that so many good qualities were shaded by Frolicks that degraded the gentleman, by weaknesses that too much betrayed the frailty of human nature!'

THOMAS LEGH AND THE REVIVAL OF LYME

In June 1792 Lord Torrington described Lyme as 'all waste and ill-keeping', and although his words were no doubt partly coloured by having been brusquely refused admittance by Colonel Legh's housekeeper, the house and park must have been a fairly sorry place in the late 18th century after the neglect of Peter the Younger's last years and his nephew's depredations. It was, however, to be comprehensively revived under Thomas Peter Legh's eldest natural son, Thomas (1792–1857), to whom the estates were bequeathed. Thomas Legh was a traveller, collector and Egyptologist who had set sail for Greece in 1811 when aged only nineteen and had assisted, 'both by his purse and his active personal exertions', according to his obituary in the *Manchester Guardian*, with the excavation and removal of the frieze from the Temple of Apollo at Bassae (now in the British Museum). He went on to Egypt, obtaining some Coptic papyri (now in the British Library) en route, and reached Ibrim in Nubia, which was further up the Nile than any European had previously travelled. Thomas Legh's *Narrative of a Journey in Egypt and the Country beyond the Cataracts* (1816) describes his travels, during which he survived crocodiles, musket balls, plague, sand storms and near-asphyxiation in the underground chambers at Amabdi. In November 1813 he returned to England to celebrate his coming-of-age and to be elected MP for Newton, which he represented until it was disenfranchised under the Reform Act of 1832. He was in Naples in February 1815 and in Brussels on the eve of Waterloo, taking part in the battle as an extra aide-de-camp to the Duke of Wellington. In 1818 he returned to the Aegean and, wearing the Ottoman dress in which he was later to be painted by William Bradley, he journeyed to Palmyra and Baalbec and to Petra, where he made the first survey of the ruins.

As soon as he came of age, Thomas Legh made use of his enormous income, estimated in 1814 to be £30,000 per annum, to overhaul the hopelessly awkward and outdated internal layout of the house, which had resulted from piecemeal development. According to the Rev. W. Marriott in 1810, the

(Left)
Thomas Legh (1792–
1857) in the eastern dress
he wore while exploring
sites around the Dead Sea
in 1818; by William
Bradley (Grand Staircase)

(Right)
William, 1st Lord
Newton (1828–98), who
created the present garden;
by George Richmond,
1878 (Grand Staircase)

principal apartments were 'immured by the dark-some approximation of garden walls, yew trees and heaths'. In 1813 the architect Lewis Wyatt, then working at nearby Tatton in succession to his uncle Samuel, had provided plans for a temporary pavilion in the courtyard to celebrate Thomas Legh's coming-of-age, and the following year he surveyed the house in readiness for undertaking alterations. Between 1814 and about 1818 he con-nected all the first-floor state rooms by rebuilding and raising the level of the east front, added a more substantial dining-room in place of Richard Legh's New Parlour, created a library out of a jumble of spaces in the south-east corner and reconstructed the Stag Parlour at a higher level. The decoration was deliberately 17th-century in character, with prominence given to the family's heraldry. Wyatt

also altered the Long Gallery and the adjoining bedrooms, added an attic tower behind Leoni's portico and put up the Gibbons carvings in the Saloon. There is, in fact, scarcely a space at Lyme which Wyatt did not touch, even parts of the hallowed Elizabethan Drawing Room being attributable to him. Yet he did his work with such sensitivity that it is often extremely difficult to tell his work from that which already existed.

Thomas Legh married twice. His first wife, Ellen Turner, was an heiress who had been abducted in 1826 by the fortune hunter and future colonial promoter, Edward Gibbon Wakefield. As a JP for Cheshire, Thomas Legh tried the famous court case that followed, and two years later married Ellen. The marriage did not produce a surviving male heir and as he had no further children by his second wife, Maud Lowther, Lyme passed, on his death in 1857, to his nephew. Prior to inheriting, William John Legh (1828–98) had served in the Crimea as a captain in the Royal Scots Fusiliers and had taken part in the Battle of Inkerman. In 1859, having returned to England and resigned his commission, he was elected one of the MPs for South Lancashire, and he subsequently represented East Cheshire, retiring from politics in 1885 and being raised to the peerage in 1892 as Baron Newton of Newton-in-Makerfield. His personal modesty and the long-held pride of the family in their status as great commoners made his acceptance of the honour something of a surprise, but, according to his son, 'he explained in a semi-apologetic manner that it was cheaper to become a peer than to serve as High Sheriff, which would otherwise have been his fate'.

The 1st Lord Newton was responsible for creating the garden much as it is today, with the advice of the landscape architect Edward Kemp, who had trained under Paxton at Chatsworth and is

best known for his writings and for laying out public parks in the north-west. Lord Newton also employed the otherwise scarcely known Manchester architect Alfred Darbyshire to undertake repairs to the house and to improve the estate buildings. A new stable block was built in 1863 on the site suggested by Wyatt nearly 50 years earlier, Wyatt's orangery was completed, and numerous other buildings were added, including more substantial replacements for the early 19th-century single-storey lodges.

THE 20TH CENTURY

Thomas Wodehouse, 2nd Lord Newton (1857–1942), who succeeded in 1898, had initially pursued a diplomatic career, serving as an attaché in the Paris Embassy from 1881, but in 1886 had been elected MP for Newton. Continuing to play an active role when in the House of Lords, he was Paymaster-General and then Assistant Under-Secretary of State for Foreign Affairs during the First World War. He was a master of the art of cultivated philistinism, disconcerting his visitors by telling them not to believe that the carvings in the Saloon were by Grinling Gibbons and letting it be known that he preferred grilled herrings to the *sole au vin blanc* lovingly prepared by his accomplished French chef, M. Perez. His vivacious and pretty wife, Evelyn Caroline, who was the first English-woman to be painted by J. Singer Sargent, was more openly proud of the house, writing two books on its history, but she shared her husband's dislike of vulgarity and display. Although central heating and electricity were introduced at Lyme shortly after the turn of the century and the fashionable Edwardian decorators Philippe and Amadée Joubert were extensively employed, Lord and Lady Newton nevertheless lovingly cherished, and sometimes even enhanced, any feature which reflected the ancientness of the house or the distinction of the family. They referred to Lyme as being Elizabethan rather than of any other period and they continued the practice begun by Lewis Wyatt of painting plasterwork, pieces of furniture and even mahogany doors to simulate dark oak – the wood which most clearly expressed

(Above) The Lyme Kitchen, about 1900–10

ancient Englishness. Lyme's vibrant Indian summer in the years immediately before the First World War – with large house and shooting parties, numerous contented children, visiting politicians and royalty and the overriding, passionate enthusiasm of Lady Newton – is brought to life by her daughter, Phyllis Sandeman, in *Treasure on Earth*, her charming record of Christmas there in 1906.

In 1920 Lord Newton made Lyme over to his son Richard, an act of enormous sacrifice, particularly for Lady Newton, which was made in an attempt to save the estate in the face of increasingly onerous taxation and rising wages. Extensive land sales had been made the previous year to provide capital, and further sales followed in the 1920s, but after the requisition of the Lancashire coal mines in 1939, the estate no longer had the support of what had been, since the mid-18th century, one of

its most important sources of revenue. Unable to obtain sufficient staff to maintain the place after the Second World War, the 3rd Lord Newton, as Richard Legh had become on the death of his father in 1942, handed Lyme and 1,323 acres of park and moorland to the National Trust in 1946 in order to secure its future. A further 56 acres at the heart of the estate were acquired from North West Water in 1995. Lyme was at first run by Stockport Corporation (later Metropolitan Borough Council), which undertook extensive structural repairs in the 1970s and the 1980s and continues to provide an important part of the funding. Since 1994 the estate has been under the direct management of the National Trust, which has continued the repairs, particularly to the park buildings. The Leghs, although no longer resident, still maintain close links with Lyme, with which they have now been associated for 600 years.